Daily Readings
with
George MacLeod

Daily Readings
with
George MacLeod

Ron Ferguson (ed)

WILD GOOSE PUBLICATIONS

Contents

Introduction

The Revd Dr George Fielden MacLeod (Very Revd Lord MacLeod of Fuinary) was one of the great figures in the tempestuous history of the Church of Scotland.

He was born in 1895 into Scotland's most notable ecclesiastical dynasty. The MacLeods of Fuinary in Morvern have given more than 550 years of ordained service to the Church. His great-grandfather was one of the great Gaelic scholars of his generation, and his grandfather, the Revd Dr Norman MacLeod of the Barony Church in Glasgow, was a confidant of Queen Victoria, friend of David Livingstone and Florence Nightingale, and one of the best known Scots of his day.

George's father was a Unionist MP, and his mother the daughter of a wealthy Lancashire cotton merchant. Sir John MacLeod, MP, sent his son to Winchester to learn to be an 'English' gentleman. The time at Winchester, where he was a contemporary of Oswald Mosley – 'a dull chap' was his verdict on the man who was to found the British Union of Fascists – reinforced his sense of privilege. He was confirmed as an Anglican. In 1913 he went to Oxford to study law.

With the outbreak of the First World War in 1914, George enlisted as an officer in the Argyll and Sutherland Highlanders. He saw service in Salonika and at the Western Front, winning the Military Cross and the Croix de Guerre for bravery. His war record was particularly pleasing to his father, who had been the head recruiter of young men in the West of Scotland.

The war had a profound effect on the young officer who had witnessed the slaughter of so many of his friends and companions. He had a conversion experience in a railway carriage on his way back to the Front. He later recounted that he had been gambling a great deal and was going through half a bottle of whisky and fifty cigarettes a day. Realising that he was 'going to hell in a hurry', he had knelt down in the railway compartment and yielded his life to Christ.

After the war, he decided to train for the ministry of the Church of Scotland. Following theological study in Edinburgh and America, and a short spell as a missionary in Canada, he became assistant minister of the prestigious St Giles' Cathedral in Edinburgh's Royal Mile. The handsome, aristocratic young Presbyterian-turned-Anglican-turned-Presbyterian was an immediate hit, and a bright future was predicted by the experienced spotters of future Moderators of the Kirk.

George left St Giles' to become first full-time Scottish padre of Toc H, the post-war Christian fellowship established by Tubby Clayton. MacLeod had met Clayton in New York, and had been greatly impressed by his drive and vision. Impatient to see new forms of church life which would provide dynamic post-war spiritual leadership, George was disappointed by Toc H's refusal to celebrate intercommunion amongst its members. He disagreed profoundly with its view that they should respect the disciplines of each church – George argued vigorously that the old disciplines were precisely what was hindering the spiritual renewal of the country. Finding himself heavily outvoted, he left the full-time service of the movement. Toc H had been formative for his thinking as he grappled with the implications of the post-war situation.

In 1926 he became associate minister of St Cuthbert's Church in the West End of Edinburgh. The charismatic and dashing young minister soon had people queuing up to hear him preach. The new darling of the ecclesiastical establishment established a reputation as an orator – a reputation enhanced by his frequent radio broadcasts to Britain and the Empire.

While in Edinburgh, he was disturbed by his increasing awareness of 'two nations', the rich and the poor. The St Cuthbert's Church mission in a poor area of the city brought him into daily contact with grinding poverty and hardship, and he became disillusioned with the post-war rhetoric about a land 'fit for heroes'. In 1930 he shocked many of his admirers – who expected him to graduate to the Moderator's chair by way of another prestigious Edinburgh charge – by becoming minister of Govan Parish Church in Glasgow.

Govan, well known as a shipbuilding area, suffered from severe unemployment in the Hungry Thirties. People crowded into the slums, and George MacLeod was touched by their plight. The poverty and depression caused him to review the privileged assumptions with which he had grown up, and also to question the basis of the First World War. The son of the Tory MP and war recruiter moved inexorably towards socialism and pacifism in the Depression years. He also moved from the straightforward high Presbyterianism of the MacLeod dynasty towards a more mystical and cosmic and even political theology.

The major turning point came in April 1933. Overwork, and the realisation that the old foundations of his life were crumbling, had led to a breakdown of health in Govan. He went out to Jerusalem to recover, and while there he took part in the Russian Orthodox early morning Easter service. He had intended to go for half an hour, and stayed for three and a half hours.

'Only eight priests took part,' he noted breathlessly in his journal, 'and a hidden choir, but they were all quite perfect. They have the supreme gift of drama, and all had perfect voices. It was really the same service as at the

Sepulchre, but done by perfect artists. When the Patriarch was heard arriving, the gates of the sanctuary were flung open and two young priests, with flowing hair and beards, rushed out to meet him – the choir sang Responses – Actions – they all entered the sanctuary – they all rushed out – Christ is Risen – candles! Quick procession – every movement was sprightly. Out of the church we all ran behind them – lighted candle in our hands – round the church three times singing, in the crisp star-laden night. Here was the answer to modern criticism! Of course Christ had risen!

'Levitation? … Physical? Subjective? … Objective? These were all meaningless words. *Christ has risen* was the sheer obvious fact! Back into the church, the two young people sang to the Patriarch. He replied in song and beautiful movements of hand and head – the two priests took the incense and swept through the congregation (not a large one) censing us and telling each one that Christ had risen – back to the centre – whenever a priest finished his part, out rang the heavenly choir, while some new "formation" was taken up by the priests. Not one had a book, not one took a "cue", and yet for three and a half hours it went on without a pause in the centre of the church.'

The service changed his view of worship.

'For sheer worship I have never seen anything like it – nor shall see again on earth. We can never touch it in the West; not even Rome could do it. It was the devotional presentation of the New Life, beyond 'Acting' and beyond 'Lesson' – simply Worship. It was the earnest that Bolshevism must pass. There was more Reality in the Patriarch's little finger than in Stalin's whole council assembled.'

Walking back to his hotel in the early morning, George told his companions that he had discovered worship for the first time. He said he had found the worship utterly evangelical, producing in people's eyes 'such a light as Moody and Sankey might produce after saying "Jesus saves" sixty times.'

It is worth quoting at length from that Jerusalem Easter journal, because it provides a key to the understanding of George MacLeod's deep sense of worship. Back in grimy Govan, rejuvenated, he searched around for theological resources to help him understand what was happening to him. As a romantic conservative radical, he found Celtic theology, as exemplified in Saint Columba of Iona, to be very illuminating. In a speech to a symposium on youth, he argued that some answers for the plight of Presbyterian Scotland could be found 'back where Scottish worship first began, in the Celtic Church of St Columba'.

Pleading for symbol, beauty and ritual in public worship, he argued that he was being true to the intention of the founding fathers of the Reformation.

'If we would be patient, we can discover here the link that saves the chain,' he said. 'For it was a return to the simple primitive Catholic Church which was the desire and purpose of the first Reformers. How many who today evoke the name of John Knox really know the things for which he stood? – frequent communion; read prayers from a liturgy; daily service in the churches; the reciting of the Apostles' Creed in worship; the response of the people to prayers; the offering of praise from the Communion Table; the pronouncing of the Benediction from the Communion Table.

'How many of these acts today – when they are enacted in a Scottish church – are called "mere aping of another church"? And yet they are in reality the things which John Knox practised in his endeavour to recover for Scotland her ancient primitive faith. Perhaps the first Reformers are to be vindicated at last, in coming days, by a return to what they sought.'

These were bold words from a Scottish Presbyterian minister in 1934. He was arguing for 'Catholic' practices, and using the authority of the great Protestant Reformers to bolster his claims! Not lacking in audacity, George MacLeod was seeking to make sense of Catholicism and Orthodoxy within a Presbyterian framework, and using the ancient kinship between Celtic theology and Eastern Orthodoxy as a linchpin.

In the meantime, he launched a wide-ranging parish mission in Govan, ensuring that every home in the area was visited. The mission produced converts and new members. His pastoral ministry was exhausting and costly, as was his deep concern for the community. He invited unemployed craftsmen to help rebuild a ruined mill outside Glasgow as a place to which Govan families could retreat for a holiday in the country; the experiment taught him many lessons. He found that unemployed men could find again their dignity in such a project, and he discovered that many men could talk more easily over a common physical task than in a seminar. In the mutual purposeful sharing of rebuilding a ruin, community was formed.

George MacLeod, who was made a Doctor of Divinity by Glasgow University in 1937, determined to make an even bigger and bolder experiment. He felt that the Church of Scotland was failing to provide trained recruits for the inner city slums and new housing estates, and he decided to embark on an innovative venture which would seek to meet the needs of the times. In 1938 he dramatically left the security of the parish ministry in Govan to begin the rebuilding of the ruined living quarters of the ancient Iona Abbey and to found the Iona Community.

Why Iona? George had often gone there on holiday as a child, and been entranced by the island and its story. He had been taught how Saint Columba had sailed from Ireland to the Scottish Hebridean island of Iona in 563, there founding a mission which had been responsible for many conversions ranging all the way from mainland Scotland to the steppes of Russia. The young George MacLeod had been entranced by the stories of the Celtic saint and his barefoot monks. He had learned how Iona had become sacred ground, one of the holy places of European pilgrimage, and how many Scottish and Norwegian kings – including, it was believed, Macbeth and Duncan – had been borne to the island for burial.

George had been taught how, once the Celtic flame had burned low, the Benedictine order had built the Abbey on the Columban site, and how the Abbey had fallen into disrepair after the Reformation. In 1899 the ruins had been handed over to the Church of Scotland by the Duke of Argyll, with the far-seeing proviso that any Christian denomination should be allowed to worship there. The Abbey church was restored by 1910 – Sir John MacLeod, MP, was one of the fundraisers – but the rest of the building lay in ruins.

When he used to go to Iona on holiday from Govan, George would look at the ruins – and found them looking back at him, asking a fundamental question. His answer was to embark on the rebuilding, using young ministers as labourers for the craftsmen as part of a training programme for industrial ministry.

Thus the controversial Iona Community was formed. They were accused of playing at monks, of escaping from the realities of life, and of playing politics. 'Half way towards Rome and half way towards Moscow' was the jibe. During the Second World War, the pacifist MacLeod, whose courage could not be questioned, was jeered at. The once popular radio preacher was silenced by the BBC.

Controversy and MacLeod were never far away from each other. As the Iona Community grew after the war and attracted visitors from all over the world, Dr MacLeod (he declined to use his inherited title, saying he wished to be known 'by the sufficient title of Reverend') became a prominent figure on the international church scene. He made frequent overseas trips to give lectures and raise funds. He was the first Presbyterian since the seventeenth century to be Select Preacher at Cambridge and to occupy the pulpit of St Paul's Cathedral. In 1954 he became the first Fosdick Visiting Professor at Union Theological Seminary, New York. In 1956 he was appointed a chaplain to the Queen, and the following year he became the sixth member of the MacLeod dynasty to become Moderator of the General Assembly of the Church of Scotland.

MacLeod's Iona Community grew to embrace lay men and women, and people from a variety of churches, including the Roman Catholic Church. Its members were bound together by a five-fold discipline of prayer, meeting together, economic sharing, planning of time and work for justice and peace. George MacLeod himself continued to be Scotland's most celebrated turbulent priest, causing controversy with his pleas for a limited form of episcopacy in the Church of Scotland, for the restoration of some kind of confessional, and for pacifism. He corresponded with Archbishops, denounced torturing regimes, pleaded for disarmament, inveighed against world hunger and advocated joint ecumenical action on social issues.

With the completion of the restoration of Iona Abbey, he resigned the leadership of the Iona Community in 1968, becoming the first Presbyterian minister to sit in the House of Lords, as the Very Revd Lord MacLeod of Fuinary. Supported by his wife, Lorna, he continued his ministry. He became president of the International Fellowship of Reconciliation, and was elected Lord Rector of Glasgow University in 1968. He continued to travel and lecture abroad, and at the age of 91, while in New York, he was awarded the Union Medal.

In 1988, during the celebrations of the Iona Community's jubilee, a new international youth and reconciliation centre on Iona was named in George MacLeod's honour. The following year, he was made joint winner of the Templeton International Prize for progress in religion. He immediately announced that the £125,000 prize money would be divided between work for peace and work for the relief of hunger.

All of this indicates a very full life of activity, controversy and influence; indeed, George MacLeod was probably best known internationally as a prophet, peacemaker and social activist, and the obituaries after his death in 1991 concentrated on these aspects of his life. Yet his pastoral and priestly roles have been at least as important.

As a preacher and leader of worship, George MacLeod had few peers. The spine-tingling oratory was well-rehearsed, but it was no mere technique. It represented the dammed-up eloquent outpourings of a man fired by the love of Christ, and his sermons changed lives, many lives. Both his public and his private challenge led many into the ordained ministry, and inspired countless people to do exceptional things with their lives. Pastorally, he would go to extreme lengths to help people, particularly delinquent boys, alcoholics and down-and-outs.

His prayers show an inspired Celtic poet at work. The language is beautiful and striking, imaginative and challenging. He would work for five hours on a five-minute prayer, refining and refining. Worship, he said, represented God's 'worthship', and only the best should be offered up to God. To be led in worship in Iona Abbey by George MacLeod was to be brought to the very gates of heaven.

At the heart of George MacLeod's theology is the Incarnation, the doctrine that in Christ God himself had entered the world's pain in love. This is the key to the understanding of his worship and politics. As he put it: 'What I find in the Bible – which differentiates our faith from all other world religions – is precisely that God is to be found in the material. And that He came to redeem man, soul and body. The Gospel claims the key to all material issues is to be found in the mystery that Christ came in a body, and healed bodies and fed bodies, and that he died in a body, and rose in a body: to save man body and soul.

'Christ is the key to every mortal thing.'

Doctrine for George was not a static statement, but a sign of living experience, which in turn led on to other unpredictable experiences.

'Christ is a person to be trusted, not a principle to be tested,' he wrote. 'The Church is a movement, not a meeting house. The faith is an experience, not an exposition. Christians are explorers, not mapmakers.'

Like Teilhard de Chardin, he saw the universe as God's cathedral, pointing to the glory of God. He linked Celtic mysticism to modern science, seeing the material order as being shot through with the Spirit. This might have degenerated into a lovey-dovey 'nice' pantheism, but, though he did not care much for Calvinism, this nevertheless son of Calvin could not be seduced into thinking that everything was basically fine. He kept reminding that Satan was let loose in the world too, and that angels needed to be called in to help in the fight against evil principalities and powers.

In all of this personal and cosmic mysticism, he was a true Celt, reverencing the earth yet crusading against evil, both personal and corporate. His vision was always a whole one – personal, corporate, political, cosmic. The total Gospel.

In personal terms, the man who knelt down in the railway carriage to welcome Christ into his heart was an evangelical all his life, with an almost childlike faith. He believed deeply in the unconditional offer of salvation, addressed to all people, everywhere. Those who caricature George MacLeod simply as a politician do not know their man. His political convictions sprang not from ideology – he was opposed to the Marxist programme and kept warning that Communism would collapse under the weight of its own wishful thinking – but from the Gospel call to justice, allied with his own knowledge of what poverty did to people. His pacifism was a direct outcome of his commitment to the Way of the Cross.

Though no systematic theologian, George MacLeod was a prophet ahead of his time. In the 1940s he predicted the environmental crisis, and called attention to ecological issues – all springing from his vision of the cosmos as the sphere of the Holy Spirit. His intuitive 'seeing' led him to prefigure some of the themes of Process theology and Liberation theology, even when he himself did not fully understand the full implications of what he was saying. As master storyteller and poet, he did not need to spell it all out: his job was to point and point and point until, like the rest of Creation, we too can cry, 'Glory.'

This selection of extracts from George MacLeod's writings is not intended as a reader in his theology. Yet they give a flavour of the thinking of the mystical man of action whose theology was not worked out in the study but on the

17

run, out on the street. It was precisely on that High Street that George saw the Spirit of God most actively at work.

I have taken some liberties with the text, but not too many I hope, to make the readings accessible for devotional purposes. I have retained George's use of 'man' and 'mankind'; in the use of such language, he was a man of his time and it did not seem right to alter the text.

This is no ordinary book of quiet devotional readings – the passion and poetry of the man, as well as his insistence that God is Here and God is Now, make that thankfully impossible. If this little book quickens devotion, loosens tongues of praise and causes divine disturbance, its purpose will have been well served.

Thanks are due to the Iona Community for permission to quote the material listed. Readers who wish to dip into the George MacLeod treasury of prayers and poetry should obtain *The Whole Earth Shall Cry Glory*, published by Wild Goose Publications.

Ron Ferguson

Prescript

A boy threw a stone at the stained-glass window of the Incarnation. It nicked out the 'E' in the word HIGHEST in the text GLORY TO GOD IN THE HIGHEST. Thus, till unfortunately it was mended, it read, GLORY TO GOD IN THE HIGH ST.

At least the mended E might have been contrived on a swivel so that in a high wind it would have been impossible to see which way it read.

Such is the genius, and the offence, of the Christian revelation.

Holiness, salvation, glory are all come down to earth in Jesus Christ our Lord. Truth is found in the constant interaction of the claim that the apex of the Divine Majesty is declared in Christ's humanity.

The Word of God cannot be dissociated from the Action of God. As the blood courses through the body, so the spiritual is alone kept healthy in its interaction in the High Street. God's revelation of Himself was not a series of mighty acts done to Israel, but a series performed in and through Israel as a community in the totality of its life.

Only One Way Left, p64

Section one

THE WAY TO GOD

The Life of Life

How do you get in touch with God?

You can't get in touch with God by creating a religious vacuum in which, as it were, to meet Him. It is more true to say that you can't get out of touch with God every moment that you live, for the simple reason that He is Life: not religious life, nor Church life, but the whole life that we now live in the flesh.

You can only contact God in the concrete now. How do you come into the presence of God?

Well, God is a spirit. No one has seen Him at any time. God is love, and love is never static, it is always outgoing. So you won't find the presence of God by seeking to achieve it in a pause. He is Reality: Love: Life: and you can't touch life. You can touch expressions of life. You can't grasp life.

And God is the Life of life.

Sermon on Prayer, July 1955

God is Now

It is necessary to recover our sense of God as Now. This in turn may sound so obvious that we must give it the content we intend. If, for the medievalist, God was There, to be aspired to, He was also Then, some day to be arrived at.

Thus the monk was the type of full holiness. By his permanent vows of enclosure he was already in the heavenly place: thus the carving in the choir and sanctuary of the abbeys concerned angels and heavenly scenes. The carvings on the screen, the partition that enclosed sanctuary and choir and faced the laity in the nave, were classically of Christ's life on earth. So to say, only the utterly committed were in heaven, the rest had to think of heaven as somewhere 'there' in the future.

But it is of the essence of the evangelistic offer that there are no longer two ways about it. Once more the modern Christian, to deal with the burden of the now, must accept the offer of God's Now: His presence in the world.

Only One Way Left, p157

Benediction of a Day

To take a natural analogy, there is a living flower. You want to have it, so you pluck it. But, by your act of plucking, it dies.

You are fascinated by a sparkling running stream, a living stream of water. But, if you grasp it, it runs through your fingers, you scoop it into a pail, you no longer have life, but just a bucket of H_2O.

There is a sunbeam dancing in your room, life from the sun. If you pull down the curtain to capture the beam, it is gone.

There is a bracing wind that enlivens your whole being. But try to catch it in a bag and you have stagnant air. All this reminds us how not to get in touch with life.

Here is the root trouble of our lives. We all love life, but the moment we try to hold it, we miss it. The fact that things change and move and flow is their life. Try to make them static and you die of worry.

This is just as true of God who is the Life of life. The only way to achieve a sense of God's presence is to put yourself in the way of Him. In our analogy, you achieve a sense of life in the presence of a flower, by a running stream, in a bracing wind, with sunbeams falling on the stream. You come home to say you have had a perfectly lovely day, which means a lively day. It has been a benediction of a day.

You can only achieve a sense of God in a similar way ... You can only find God in the now.

Sermon on Prayer, July 1955

In Christ is Yea

You can only find God in the 'now'.

There is an attractive group of Buddhists in Japan who seek to make this point – the Zen Buddhists. They have monasteries to which tired businessmen come to get in touch with God again.

The monks have a fascinating way of showing that these men are always in touch with God. Here are some snatches of conversation.

'Ever since I came here,' complained a businessman, 'no one has instructed me in the meaning of reality.'

'But,' said the monk, 'I've been instructing you all the time.'

'In what way?'

'Well, when you brought me tea, did I not accept it? When you made bows to me, did I not return them? When did I ever neglect to instruct you?'

Seeing the businessman did not understand, the monk said, 'If you want to see, see directly into it. If you try to think about it, it is altogether missed.'

Another man asked, 'What is reality?' The monk replied, 'Walk on.'

'What is realisation?' asked another. A monk replied, 'Your everyday thoughts.'

'What is the ultimate word of truth?' asked another. The monk said, 'Yes.'

'What is the ultimate word of truth?' the man shouted. Monk: 'I am not deaf.'

Another asked, 'What are the characteristic features of your school of thought?' The monk replied, 'A table, a tray, a chair, a fireplace and a window.'

'What is the religious life?' – 'In the early morning, good morning: and at night, good night.'

All this is a subtle way of saying where God is contacted. Of saying, 'God is right now, or not at all.' Life is right now, or not at all.

Of course, we Christians can go further. God is spirit, and no one has seen Him at any time: but we believe Jesus Christ has declared Him.

In Christ we know what life is about: we are to walk on to a goal we know. Our everyday thoughts are what He came to change.

But He does so in ordinary life: among the tables and trays and chairs and windows that surround our lives: the innumerable contacts that form our ever-lasting nows.

The one ultimate word of truth is Yes. In Christ is Yea: He has visited and redeemed His people. But the place of His presence is not in the Then but in the Now.

Sermon on Prayer, July 1955

Primitive Holiness

A great difficulty for prayer is our difference from medieval man, when so many of our 'aids to prayer' stem from a medieval pattern. I have what I call a 'bankrupt corner' in my library and I am, if negatively, encouraged to discover it on the manse shelves of most ministers who have tried to pray. It is a platoon of Bantam booklets enlisted at intervals to help one to pray better: purchased, as each severally went dead on us, on the principle that 'hope springs eternal'.

Why do they go dead on us? Because most of them are written in terms of a different consciousness. Because most of them are conceived in medieval terms, we are not really conditioned to read what they are really saying. For medieval man life was dull, brutish and short. Life here was over against the real life of the Spirit. Indeed the Greek conception of the Spirit dominated their thought forms as Thomas Aquinas was dominated by Aristotle. For the Greeks, the Spirit was over against the body, while for the Hebrew the residence of the Spirit was in the blood.

We moderns are of a different expectancy. Life is not brutish or short. We are girt about with possibilities. If medieval man looked up through a telescope, we rather look down through a microscope. Matter is so marvellous. If his fears were ghosts in the heavenlies, ours are in the infinitesimal but infernal and paradoxically infinite possibilities of hydrogen.

Modern man is earthed, materially environed. Our devotions are transmuted. There is no advance in all this. We are enmeshed in this materialism. But the secret of our exit is of vast importance. 'Back to devotionalism' would be as fatal as if our agricultural community went 'back to the land' by selling their tractors and yoking bullocks to the plough.

As it must be forward to the land, so it must be forward to the new devotionalism: or rather, to the recovery of primitive holiness. The key is in a serious review of the challenge of the Incarnation.

Only One Way Left, pp151–2

God Comes Down and In

The Bible offer superbly suits our modern need.

The Bible offer is that God comes down and God comes in. This is supremely what the New Testament is about.

The Old Testament Jews for centuries had been making the finest effort yet to get in touch with God. All the temple paraphernalia to get near God. And for all their purging and illumining they just could not get the united experience: unity with God.

So God acted. God acted at Christmas. In the superb words of an ancient prayer: 'While all things were in quiet silence at Bethlehem, and that night was in the midst of her swift course, Thine Almighty Word leaped down out of Thy Royal Throne: Hallelujah!'

That is the symbol placed in Bethlehem of what is happening: whenever you and I want it to happen. 'If we being evil know how to give good gifts to our children, how much more will the heavenly Father give the Holy Spirit to them that ask Him?'

We don't have to climb to God, or circle the world with intellectual flight or devotional achievement. God comes down and God comes in. Nearer indeed than the LCC Hall to the House of Commons: not even a bridge between: closer is He than breathing, nearer than hands and feet.

We have been given union with God, whether we like it or not, know it or not, want it or not. Our flesh is His flesh and we can't jump out of our skins. It isn't pantheism. It is a free spontaneous gift of the living God.

And it happened for everyone.

Modern Man and Prayer, sermon July 1955

The Royal Road?

When the Church got enmeshed in a pagan state after Constantine in the third century, the best among the Christians fled from so much materialism. Unfortunately they left that frying pan to land in the fire. They went to the deserts of Egypt and met the streams of mysticism that rooted from the Eastern faiths with their denial of the body. And from that contact grew up a form of mysticism alien to the incarnation faith which, none the less, like ivy, battened on the pristine oak, and still enmeshes our idea of holiness. They introduced the Via Negativa: the way of interior denial. Unfortunately, the Via Negativa cuts dead across the Emmaus Road.

It is in this uneasy situation that we come, from the little books on spirituality, to suppose that the prayer life is a series of rarefied spiritual exercises, if by any means we can attain. We must, they say, go through what the mystics called the purgative experience, forcing from our minds what is unclean. We must then be open to the illuminative experience lest seven devils enter into the heart made clean. Finally, if we practise enough, we may be granted the unitive experience when in a selfless stillness we know ourselves in the Presence.

They are daunting instructions. Laboriously followed, we have known them to lead on to what seemed like an achievement when, usually, on turning to the next stage in expectation, the instructor warns us that what we feel we have experienced is certainly bogus!

That such experiences, in more disciplined obedience, have some validity it would be blasphemous to deny. But I am convinced that few have the psychic capacity for such flights. I dare the further claim that such excursions are not even the royal road to holiness within the Christian dispensation, though we may be sure they are paths accepted by the Father of our Lord.

Yet how many earthbound mortals have departed almost completely from a serious prayer life because they thought such the essence of prayer, and are benumbed by their failure to attain. Again, and it is here that I question it as the royal road, how many who genuinely attain in fact keep on that knife-edge of practical obligation that is the urgent need of our time? So delectable, if demanding, is the exercise that they are apt to cut off the telephone when a whole world is trying to get through to them in the extremity of our need. None the less, it is these whom we are inclined to suppose are the truly religious, or the really spiritual.

Only One Way Left, pp152–3

The Straight Way

Many of us, feeling we are not made for the spiritual life, embrace the practical, and slither on to the knife-edge walk without sufficient prayer. We dismiss the Bantam platoon of books on spirituality, so constant now is the telephone. We comparably degenerate just at the moment when, if we seriously recovered the pristine holiness, we might have the word for our world.

There remain the cross-benchers who become hardly dependable for either school. Now practical, now spiritual, their telephone just ceases to ring. Neither to conduct a retreat nor lead a war on want are they fitted.

We are immersed in the here and now. We know that we must be. But too often when we turn to prayer, the isolation intensifies, the medieval resurrects and neither life becomes powerful nor prayer real. Such is the problem in personal terms. We are each a reflection of our scene. As of the microcosm so of the macrocosm, we are a replica of our society; where the oratories are too empty of life and the laboratories too filled with the potentialities of death.

The key perhaps is this: if we are to come level with the modern demands of the Incarnation, we must take more seriously the full offer that resides in the doctrine. Personally consumed of the here and now, we must discover the sense of God as Here and Now.

This is to recall the evangelical offer over the medieval. It is to short-circuit the laborious stages of the purgative, the illuminative and the unitive: or to invert them.

But first of all it is to knock away again the props from the Scala Sancta, that stair of so sincere but fruitless an approach which Martin Luther grasped a saw to sever.

There are two straight ways of getting from your house to the garden gate. One is to proceed directly. There is at least in theory an alternate straight approach: it is to leave by the back door and encircle the world. Apart from the probability that you will meet with so many enticing attractions on the road that you will never get home, it is a faithless way. It is the way of noble works: and in prayer has parallel in the purgative, through the illuminative, to the unitive gate.

But the lesson of the Incarnation is that you cannot do a thing about getting nearer God. Here is the Evangel – when Israel were dead beat and weary, trying with the noblest methods yet devised to get nearer God, in the superb words of an ancient prayer of the Nativity, 'While all things were in quiet silence at Bethlehem, and that night was in the midst of her swift course, Thine Almighty Word leaped down out of Thy Royal Throne: Hallelujah!'

Only One Way left, pp155–6

Being Earthed

Anyone who has visited the funfair must know the penny-in-the-slot machine constructed to give you an electric shock.

You put in your coin and then hold on to a brass bar as long as you can stand the increasing voltage. But should you care to stand on a bit of india-rubber or any non-conducting material – if you are not earthed – you can put in a dozen pennies, still retain your grip, and watch the voltage sparking up to dizzy heights, without any feeling at all. It is not because the machine is not working: it is because you are not earthed. There is no impression where there is no expression.

How many are the individuals who rightly decide to engage in personal prayer, but wrongly take care that the answer to prayer – the power of God coming into them – is not allowed to have issue through them and out into the world. And how soon do such protest that 'the machine is not working'.

God, in fact, is answering as surely as an electric current is entering a man even though he be not earthed: but His power is simply returning to its source. The man does not feel it because he is insulated.

Conviction of power, in the life of a congregation as of an individual, depends on being earthed. We must have constant outside contact to keep alive.

One description of the Incarnation is that God deigned to become earthed. And a correct description of the Church on earth is that it is the extension of the Incarnation. But God became incarnate not to be lost in the earth, but that the world, through Him, might be saved.

We Shall Rebuild, p92

Closer than Breathing

If we, being evil, know how to give good gifts to our children, how much more will the heavenly Father give the Holy Spirit to them that ask Him? We do not have to climb to God, or circle the world, with intellectual flight or devotional excursion. He comes down and He comes in.

Nearer indeed than even the garden gate. 'Closer is He than breathing, nearer than hands and feet.' We have been given union with God, whether we like it or not, want it or not, know it or not. Our flesh is His flesh and we cannot jump out of our skins. This is not pantheism. It is not a necessary or inherent fact of our being. It is a free, spontaneous and unnecessary gift of eternal life by the living and loving God.

It happened for everyone. He took on the flesh of the whole world. God wills that all people should be saved. Our only problem is whether we are going to accept it, be bathed in it.

All we need to do is to receive Him: and 'as many as receive Him, to them He gives the power to be the same nature with God'.

Only One Way Left, p155

Going Home

When the Prodigal Son decided to go home, we read of him that 'when he came unto *himself* he said, "I will go unto my father."'

The difference between man and the beasts is that beasts, in their natural condition, are themselves. Man in his natural condition is not 'himself'. In his natural condition he is less than himself. He comes to himself, to the Humanity that was God's intention for him, only when he decides to return home. And to reach home, to become converted, to be born again, is to become a new creation, which is to be Human at last.

We Shall Rebuild, p155

The Undertaker has Been and Gone

To be incorporated in Christ (to be 'buried with Christ in baptism that we may rise with Christ to newness of life') is an affair of the 'total man': it affects our bodies as our souls, because Christ came in a body. To be incorporated therein is to have eternal life here and now ('we, too, are dead and our lives are hid with Christ in God') because Christ is in the heavenly place.

It means that so far as we are concerned the undertaker has been and gone; it is a matter of indifference to us whether at some future date anyone will or will not put a wreath of flowers on the box that contains our mortal remains.

We are already 'passed from death unto life because we have love of the brethren', already part of the New Community. 'It does not appear what we shall be, yet we know we shall be like Him, because we shall see Him as He is'; thus anyone who is so incorporated, anyone who has this hope in him, 'purifies himself as He is pure'.

We Shall Rebuild, p29

Unconditional Welcome

Christ always preached self-sacrifice in His life, and not only in His death. But the Cross, coming at the end, stands clear-cut and incisive, reflecting, as in some brilliant miniature, the larger framework of His whole life's message.

His life from start to finish was like a sun giving warmth to all who came within its rays; but in His Cross that same sun became focused, as through a lens, till the warmth of His example becomes so concentrated as to set on fire all that it touches. That resolute persistency, that doing battle with the hilt when His sword was gone ... attracts people, draws them, thrills them. You cannot say why; it is just that it does. In being lifted up He arrested the attention not of the House of Israel only, who knew His claims. He moved the very universal heart of humankind.

What is this healing power that comes from the Cross that all these hymns keep trying to express? May we say that the Cross was a dramatisation – terrible in its reality – of the parable of the prodigal Son? As we read that story of the son who went into a far country and spent his substance in riotous living, and on his return (only because he was hungry!) found the great unconditional welcome – is there anyone who doubts but that the son, when he learnt what his father was really like, surrendered, and accepted those new clothes, and lived at last in freedom in his father's house? Once he had grasped it, could he do aught else than be healed by a love like that?

And what if the Cross is a dramatisation of that which is eternally true? What if God is really like that, here and now?

Can we really go on being like this?

And it needed a Cross to tell us God is like that.

Govan Calling, pp11–12

Release from Sins

It is the agelong restlessness of the human heart to feel all right everyway, to feel free inwardly. The trouble is 'how'.

All religions might be described as different shots at 'how'. The best shot ever made in the ancient world was the Jewish attempt. They said, 'You alone can feel free. How? By obeying God's commandments.'

So they started with the Ten Commandments, but the trouble was they ended up with over a thousand commands to be obeyed in their terrifying effort to feel free. A thousand works to be performed to achieve freedom, to feel all right everyway.

But there was far worse trouble than that for those sincere and desperate Jews. After they had sincerely tried to keep the whole law they didn't feel free. No wonder they felt desperate, the finest effort yet made still having failed.

No wonder Christ had to come to so desperate a situation. He offered a new way altogether. He said, in effect, 'I'll take the sin.' As St Paul says, 'He who knew no sin became sin on our behalf that we might be, in Christ, the righteousness of God.' That we might be free, feel all right everyway, be found not guilty.

To have faith in Christ is to believe that Jesus reveals God, that is, reveals the pattern of reality for our world. It is to believe that Jesus releases us from our sins. It is to believe the future is safe in His hands, both for the rest of our lives and for our lives, too, beyond the grave.

But these are apt to be words, words, aren't they? Why? May it be because we think faith is an affair of the mind – assent to certain propositions? You see, the Bible never thought in these terms. The Bible always thinks that faith is an affair of action.

Sermon, August 1953

The Knife-Edge

There are evenings when our prayer life is refreshing: but, analysed, they turn out to be the times when the pressures have been so weighty that you have simply had to go with them to God. But this is precisely the recovery of the knife-edge. The religious moment flowers from the practical. Of the prayer life, too, we can come to say, 'Hereby we know that we are passed from death unto life, because we love the brethren.'

'The author is getting at something,' you may be saying, 'but just when I think I understand I lose contact again.' Well, the author has no doubt that, through an abler pen, the moments of lucidity would be longer and those of bemusement shorter. But I would also hazard that, with the ablest pen, you would find that you were missing and hitting it: with momentarily clear views followed by eddying mist. Such is the nature of our Citadel. For the mystery of true life is the mystery of the Word made flesh.

In the true life of prayer we are forever on the knife-edge. We move in the light and shadow of Him who is born Son of God and Son of Man. Manifestly there is a new prayer life demanded: not stationary times with God, but living, flowing times when, by His Spirit, we are exercised in unravelling the mystery of that apex of majesty which is His humanity.

Only One Way Left, pp160–1

Prayer and Pressure

It is the primacy of God as Now that we must recover in Christian mysticism, as starting point in the new holiness.

When in the morning we get to our desk … that list of meetings, the whole design of the day's life as it builds up from this or that telephone call, the person we like whom we are to meet at four, the person more difficult to like who will come at five … such is the Bren-gun rapidity of our warfare. How apt we are to wonder where God comes in! Get through the grey, we are apt to say, and then perhaps at nine o'clock tonight, or nearer perhaps to eleven, we can have our time with God!

But 'whatever wakes my heart and mind, Thy presence is, my Lord'. The great contribution of the Hebrew to religion, let us recall, is that he did away with it. Our innumerable and pedestrian 'nows' are our points of contact with God in the highest, the apex of whose majesty is in His most glorious humanity.

You may be asking, 'Is the author hinting that there need be no prayer time at all? Is he suggesting that life is sufficient prayer?' I am not. What debilitates our prayer life, I suggest, is our presupposition that the pressures of life are on one side while God is on some other side. With this presupposition, when evening comes with an ending to our pressures, we are apt to go eagerly to God – disconcertingly to find a vacuum. We seek to fill the vacuum with 'spiritual thoughts'. The more we try, the more desperate does the situation become: till in effect we say that we are not really the praying type.

Thus we begin to lean perilously to one side of the knife-edge.

Only One Way Left, p160

Preparing for the Day

It was said of a great politician that he rose at six to plot his day: not just to marshal his diary but to make his own the documents that would enlighten the flux of interview and telephone that interlaced his life. A well-known publisher, after reading his morning mail, endeavours to lock his door for half an hour and resolutely face the particular issues that are likely to go wrong instead of, like so many of us, skipping the difficult engagements that we know loom up and hoping for the best till the awkward – and unprepared for – moment arrives. Both these men attained an altitude in advance that carried them serenely through their day. Such again is for a figure. Whatever wakes our heart and mind each day is going to be the presence of the Lord.

Thus, in the morning, we resolutely count out the paper money of our plotted day till we have assessed its value in the coinage of the eternal. In the light of the Incarnation, nothing is secular. But unless we handle each paper token of the seeming secular and hold it till we see its true value in the light of the glorified humanity then, by ten of the morning, we are down one precipice of the knife-edge and are in a like judgement with the pietist who has gone down the other side.

You may rest assured that all the old disciplines of prayer come into play. It is true that we start with the unitive. We start with the acceptance of the marvellous offer of the Incarnation. But do you suppose, as we make our own such attendant thoughts as are proffered by St John of Damascus, that they do not lead us into adoration and thereafter to utter self-abasement and confusion of face?

The purgative necessity, of throwing this out from our consciousness and that from our characters, is every bit as demanding as in the older discipline. But it is no longer a disrelated spiritual exercise towards an experience.

When we have wrestled with our state and given it to Him, the illuminative becomes our urgent need and not our pious obligation. In such a mood, the Bible is not something that 'ought' to be read, but its opening becomes a sheer necessity of our condition.

Only One Way Left, pp161–2

Thanksgiving and Failure

As the day proceeds and its engagements excite us, abase, exalt, appal us, arrows of ejaculation soar up, whose feathers were adjusted earlier as we prepared for our warfare and resolutely visualised the targets that the day would bring.

When evening comes, and solemn assembly with our Lord is hard to rise to, we can go backward over the day and from this occurrence or from that it is not difficult to find reason for our thanksgiving or intercession and all too easy to recall failures that demand our penitence. It may well end with supplication that much of what became so secular today may tomorrow be transmuted a little closer to the sacramental.

Despite all, the devil will probably still get hold of us. We may find ourselves saying, 'I thank God I am not as these pietists.

'In addition to my parish visiting, I have dealt with a criminal who has ill repaid me. I have been to a United Nations meeting. I have tried to share a wider vision with a trades union official. Indeed I have been involved. I thank God I am not as one of these pietists.'

The devil will have got us once again. But of God's grace we will take the Book for a final illuminative moment. It will open at the story of a certain publican who went up to the Temple to pray.

Thus we will go to sleep in the mood in which we should always go to sleep: saying with truth, 'God be merciful to me a sinner,' and yet saying it with hope, for there is a Man in heaven.

Only One Way Left, pp162–3

Opposing Moods

When you have a dream, do you know that you are all the characters in the dream?

Let me tell you some of the things that go to make up yourself. I'm sure they do, because they make up me and everybody. Do you grasp, for instance, that you are all the characters in the Bible, save one?

For instance, I'm sure there's the legalist in you, always making laws for yourself. You are going to get up earlier. Or you resolve to answer your letters more promptly, or whatever it is.

But that's not all that there is to you by any manner of means, because you have an opposite mood, so have I – not to be worried by laws. You want to live unrestricted. You want life and beauty and music. And if you give yourself to these, you argue, then getting up and writing letters will look after themselves. Do you know that's the Greek in you, because the Greeks loved life and beauty and freedom.

But there are other facets in your make-up, aren't there? Take anything: take the defence of our land. Haven't you changing moods about that? Don't you sometimes feel: 'To blazes with it all. I've no quarrel with anyone. I want peace, and I'm going all out for it, at any cost. I'm not going to get mixed up in all the intricate arguments about the necessity of defence.' And then, the very next day, you read a moving appeal to work harder for rearmament, and you go and do it.

I suppose you know these two opposing moods are the mood of the zealot on the one hand, and the Sadducee on the other. The Nonconformist mood, and the Conformist to the powers that be. When you add these moods up and other moods besides, what a shattered, divided person you become. 'I don't know what to make of myself' – that's your summary. Or, 'I don't know what to believe.' Why? Because you are Jew and Greek and Zealot and Sadducee, all in one.

And don't you see, the Bible is precisely the dramatisation of all this?

Sermon: The Bible in History and in Life, 1952

The Inside Story

A very famous actor was once staying at a country house party. It was Sunday, and a quite unknown vicar had been asked to supper.

After some recitations the actor, to honour Sunday, was asked to recite some scripture, and he chose to recite the 23rd psalm, 'The Lord is My

Shepherd'. Everyone applauded the artistry of his rendering, and the host asked the vicar to recite the same psalm. His rendering received no response, except a silence.

The vicar was embarrassed by his seeming failure, but afterwards the actor said to him, 'Don't be depressed. You moved us greatly. You see, I know the psalm, but you know the Shepherd.'

The Bible is the most profound dramatisation of you. There they all are, Jews and Greeks and Zealots and Sadducees and the rest, all milling around Christ. As you read that outside story, you find it's your own inside story. And Christ in the story can confront the inner you that is you. Over against that gibberish of words that is your divided life, there stands the Word of God.

The historic story of Christ, the outside story of Christ, suddenly emerges as the inside story of yourself – and it is this inner story, this inner parallel, that really makes the Bible inspired so that to your condition it becomes the living Word of God.

Think when reading it, then, of all the characters and groups as instances of you, whether good or bad characters. Then read it as what God says to you, or what Christ says to you through these characters, these groups, these situations. And you will come to the great conclusion that everything is outside-in and inside-out, or, as the Bible actually says of the first preachers, they turned everything upside down.

Sermon: The Bible in History and in Life, 1952

Creation is Not Enough

Almighty God, Creator;
the morning is Yours, rising into fullness.
The summer is Yours, dipping into autumn.
Eternity is Yours, dipping into time.
The vibrant grasses, the scent of flowers, the lichen on the rocks,
the tang of seaweed,
all are Yours.
Gladly we live in this garden of Your creating.

But Creation is not enough.
Always in the beauty, the foreshadowing of decay.
The lambs frolicking careless: so soon to be led off to slaughter.
Nature red and scarred as well as lush and green.
In the garden also: always the thorn.
Creation is not enough.

Almighty God, Redeemer:
the sap of life in our bones and being is Yours:
lifting us to ecstasy.
But always in the beauty: the tang of sin in our consciences.
The dry lichen of sins long dead, but seared upon our minds.
In the garden that is each of us, always the thorn.

Yet all are Yours as we yield them again to You.
Not only our lives that You have given are Yours:
but also our sins that You have taken.
Even our livid rebellions and putrid sins:
You have taken them all away
and nailed them to the Cross!
Our redemption is enough: and we are free.

The Whole Earth Shall Cry Glory

Solidarity in Prayer

So far are we from the Hebraic mood that we can hardly understand one of their proverbs – 'When an Israelite prays, all Israel prays.' We must come not only to understand it but to make it our own.

As a Presbyterian, I often envy the techniques of Rome. One, to assist a sense of solidarity in prayer, is to remind their people that Mass is celebrated every hour of the day or night. So far-flung is their Church that dawn is breaking every hour and there and then the Offering is made. Christ is tabernacled with men, and with Him there is no distance of space or time. Thus each person anywhere can incorporate his seeming lonely act with the lonely tabernacling of our God on earth which, at that hour, is somewhere being celebrated.

For those of us bereft of such technique, it is healthy to remember that our loneliness is probably of recent date. Our immediate Presbyterian grandfathers rarely felt they prayed alone. Even if fortune took them to the colonies, conscious in their prayers was the little group then kneeling in the little cottage in the glen that they had left. A corporate commitment was the fibre of their prayer.

But we are isolated now. In such a mood we do well to remember the constant intercession in the heavenly place and, in our offering, to feel identified with Him and with all who in Him dwell. But if that be too demanding on our imagining, it is good, if only as a crutch for our frailty, to lean on some small committed group that daily pray for us as we do for them. The sense of membership of an intimate group before the throne makes less demanding the vision of the Intercessor in the midst.

Only One Way Left, p150

Divine Intoxication

God wills that all should be saved. Our only problem is whether we are going to accept it. All we have to do is to receive Him. As many as receive Him, to them He gives power to be of the same nature with God: the unitive experience.

Listen to these two short quotations from the early fathers, and see why they called the Gospel that divine intoxication more sober than sobriety itself.

Cries St Simeon: 'We become Christ's members and Christ becomes our

Member. Unworthy though I be, my hand and foot are Christ. I move my hand and my hand is fully Christ. I move my foot, and lo it glows like God Himself.' Or St John of Damascus saying the same thing: 'We hold that to the whole of human nature the whole essence of Godhead was united. He in his fullness took upon Himself me in my fullness. And was united whole to whole that He might in His grace bestow salvation on the whole man.'

Here is the validation of our social concern. Here is our interest in body healing and healing of the body politic. Here is the death of cynicism. Here is the Resurrection faith. God is here.

He is here for you alone on that bed of sickness. Christ is not 'there' to be arrived at. Say of Him in your bed – He is beside you, above you, beneath you, in you. And He is here as king, waiting to serve, if only we will serve.

Easter doesn't picture Him as standing outside conference rooms. Easter pictures Him as coming in when all the doors are shut, saying 'Peace be unto you', even while He also shows His broken side and wounded feet. He is here, always here, waiting to be availed of, waiting to be used.

What do you do now when you shut your eyes? Well, for one thing, give the real meaning to 'Amen'. It does not mean 'May it be so'. Amen means 'It is so'.

You can't do a thing about getting nearer to God. He has come down and He has come in. Whatever you pray for, believe that you have it and it will be done to you.

When you shut your eyes now, you won't open them in confusion.

When you shut your eyes now, believe that He is here, instant, available.

Sermon: Modern Man and Prayer, July 1955

Section two

THE MERCY OF GOD

Working the Gold Mine

We are not saved by works; but unless we become part of the saving work, salvation ceases to work for us.

We are indeed forgiven our trespasses, but 'if we forgive not men their trespasses neither will our Father in heaven forgive us'. We have, with other citizens of God's Kingdom, been presented with a gold mine, free gratis and for nothing. But we have still got to get picks and go and work the thing – in fear and trembling – if we are to feel enriched.

A man was once left a million pounds. The lawyer sent him a bank book and the address of the bank where the money was deposited. But he never drew a cheque and he died in rags – worth a million pounds! We must continually be involved if we are to remain in a state of salvation.

An Idea Whose Hour is Come, pp4–5

Back from the Pawnshop of Death

Christ have mercy.
You sit at the right hand of God
    interpreter of truth,
    dispenser of gifts,
    advocate of sinners.
But we dodge the truth

doubt the gifts

discount any need of Your advocacy.

Have mercy.

We glory in Your Creation, Father:

in Your buying us back from the pawnshop of death:

Christ, in Your supporting: Spirit of uplift.

But we do not make this clear to men on earth.

Rather do we grossly defile Your Creation,

lightly presume on what it costs You to win us back

till we assume that it is our zest and our jollity that keeps us high.

Have mercy.

The Whole Earth Shall Cry Glory

Factory of Forgiveness

Forgiveness is boundless, as deep as God's love comes down to us, and it has to come pretty deep to encompass me, and perhaps it has to come pretty deep to encompass you.

As deep as God's love comes down to us, so broad should our forgiveness be to our fellows.

How often forgive? Till seventy times seven. And the area of forgiveness? From the North Pole to the South, and all round the equator.

This is what the Church is, the factory of forgiveness. You call it weak? Of course it is. It is the weakness of God that is stronger than men.

You call it foolish? Of course it is, but the foolishness of God is wiser than men. The ways of the Kingdom are at war with the ways of the world.

This is not a forgiving age. And why should it be? The question we have to ask is whether the Church is a forgiving church: whether it practises enough the essential madness for which it was put into the world. Madness? Yes, and the world is sane.

And is our sane world in so happy a plight? Would it not be worth trying God's way from pole to pole and round the equator, wherever Christians are?

Sermon, August 1956

Forgiveness

What is Christian forgiveness like?

Perhaps it is summed up in the correct reading of our text: 'Forgive us our debts as we have forgiven our debtors.'

It means we cannot lay hold on our forgiveness from God unless we have put it in practice to our neighbour. Does that mean that God's forgiveness is conditional?

God is always forgiving. Whether we are aware of His forgiveness depends on our spirit, our attitude.

It is not unlike a man who might get a legacy of one million pounds. The lawyer who informs him might say it is lodged in the bank at 101 High Street, and might enclose a cheque-book. Now supposing that lucky man never used the cheque-book, never drew on his fortune. He might die of starvation, yet no one could say he was not worth a million pounds.

The truth is we are paupers if we don't keep money in circulation. We just don't know we are forgiven, unless we keep this coinage in circulation, unless we not only draw on forgiveness but share it.

Jesus says elsewhere, 'If ye forgive not men their trespasses, neither will your Father in heaven forgive you your trespasses.'

The great sin, the sin compared with which adultery is a bagatelle, is failure to forgive.

To the woman taken in adultery, he said, 'Neither do I condemn thee. Go and sin no more.' But compare this with the story he told about the man who, after having been let off a huge debt, pursued a debtor for a small sum.

What does Jesus say of that man? Does he say that he was unimaginative? Stingy? Poor spirited? No. He says of him that he is damned, finished, out. Why? Because knowing himself forgiven, he was not prepared to forgive. This is the heart of the Gospel seen from the reverse side. Seen from the positive side, it reminds us of what God has done for us.

Sermon, August 1956

Love Indeed

'God was in Christ reconciling the world unto Himself.' A medical student once told me that from the age of seventeen till his graduation he hated his father, so much did he drive him to his studies.

On the night before his graduation his father explained that when the lad was seventeen his own doctor had warned him to give up business as he might drop dead. Without capital he decided to remain at business in the hope that he would survive till his boy's graduation; but he also ensured, by driving, that the boy would not have a delayed course.

'From that moment,' said the young medic, 'I was reconciled to my father.'

Now, if we are to be honest, but for Christ's revelation of what God is really like, it would sometimes be hard to be reconciled to God. Time and again He does not seem to care for the individual. He seems a hard taskmaster. If He makes His sun to shine on the evil and the good, He seems also at times as indiscriminate in the blows He distributes to the good as to the evil.

I have never seen the problem of undeserved suffering satisfactorily answered. We can all understand the child who said, 'I love Jesus but I hate God.' But if really to see Jesus is to see God, then by faith if not by sight we are indeed reconciled to God. We see the truth of God behind the 'seeming'. No one can put into words the love of the Father as Jesus reveals it. We can only fumble with inadequate human parallels, such as the love of a mother at her best. The love of a mother consists in going on loving you whatever you do to her.

What Jesus reveals about God is indeed a catharsis, 'a purification of the emotions by vicarious experience'. God, it is revealed, does not concern Himself as to how far we hurt Him. We can proceed to crucify Him if we wish. What concerns God is how far we hurt ourselves in the process! Here is Love indeed.

Only One Way Left, p33

Crucifying Christ

There is an incident in my life that still makes me go hot and cold with shame.

I was an officer in the First World War. I was travelling on Christmas Eve to London in the last night train out of Bristol.

Three of us were playing cards in a first-class carriage. The third class were packed like sardines down the corridor. We stopped at Bath.

I could point out to you now the position in the station where our carriage stopped: there were lights there, and there. On the platform there was a seething mass of troops trying to get the last train into London for Christmas. 'Let us in, governor,' they said, their faces jammed against the window. Up came the station master. 'You men can't get in except these officers say yes.'

We were playing cards, we were comfortable. We said 'No'. And on the instant, out moved the train. At that moment we came to: we were aghast: we pulled the communication cord. It was broken.

And to my dying day I shall see the faces of the men we left to celebrate Christmas away from home.

Father, forgive us, we didn't know what we were doing. This is the sort of thing that also crucifies Christ.

I am forgiven, but I won't forget.

Sermon, August 1956

Forgiving and Forgetting

I was busy. I was writing letters. I was self-important. My little daughter was going to school that morning for the first time. She came into my room, in her first school uniform. I said, 'Your tie is not quite straight.'

Then I looked at her eyes. She wasn't crying. She was unutterably disappointed. She hadn't come for tie inspection. She had come to show she was going to school for the first time. A terrific day, and I had let her down.

What is that bit in the Gospel? Whosoever shall offend against one of these little ones … better for a millstone to be tied around his neck and that he be cast into the sea.

I ran downstairs. I said all the right things. I crossed the road with her. I went to school with her.

I had missed the moment, missed the point.

I will always see these eyes. Sometimes when I am very busy. Sometimes when I am writing letters. I am forgiven, but I won't forget.

If we want to know our forgiveness, we must unfailingly believe that we are forgiven, honest to goodness believe we are forgiven. When we do, we cannot be other than forgiving.

The fortune that streams down from the Cross makes rivulets again in the parched earth of our modernity and of our crises, and runs out for the healing of the nations.

Sermon, August 1956

Parson's Phrases

When will people realise that forgiveness belongs to the market place?

Is it our jargon, our parson's phrases, that cage forgiveness into cloisters? And confines forgiveness to church walls?

A boy of twelve came home enthusiastic from Sunday School.

'Mummy,' he said, 'we heard a wonderful story today. It was about Moses. You see, the Israelites were captive in Egypt. They decided to get out, so first of all they built up a resistance movement. Then they infiltrated behind the Egyptian lines.

'The Jews were organised into commando groups. They broke through and came to the Red Sea. But they could not get across, so they built a Bailey bridge and went over. From the other side they noticed the Egyptians were following in tanks.

'So Moses called up his air force on his walkie-talkie to bomb the bridge. Down went the bridge with the Egyptians on it, into the Red Sea.'

His mother, aghast, interrupted him. 'But is that really what you heard?'

'Yes,' said the boy.

'And was that really the way your teacher told you?' asked the mother.

'Oh no,' said the boy, 'but if I had told you in the way she put it you wouldn't have understood what I was talking about.'

Is it our Bible language that confines forgiveness to church walls?

Sermon, August 1956

Dismembering the Cross

What has recognisably happened, if the crudity can be forgiven, is that we have dismembered the Cross.

Churchmen carry around the vertical beam of Christ, and unconsciously escape the turgid demands of its corollary in horizontal obedience. (Or do we do it consciously when we glimpse the measure of the cost?) While the world (oh so moral and well meaning!) carries round the horizontal, forever seeking right relations with neighbour or nation, trying to get itself straight without the Bible knowledge about man's condition that humbles, and about the Christ that alone can totally exalt.

Because it is not 'engaged', the Faith becomes vacuous. Because it is blind, the world can never glimpse the only way to peace.

It is precisely the conjunction of the vertical and the horizontal that, in every sense, makes the Cross. And it is the Cross alone that can save.

Only One Way Left, p37

Section three

THE SPIRITUAL
& THE MATERIAL

Christ the Key

What really is the Gospel?

Is it really the declaration of a spiritual world over against a material world?

Is it really that this physical world is a vale of woe, and we must keep our spirits clean so as to bear up in it and finally find freedom in heaven?

Is it that this material world is doomed to destruction, but there is a way of escape even in this life, and happy are they that find it?

Is it that the physical, the earthly, is of very passing account whether it be physical bodies, or physics or bodies-politic, and that matter does not matter, while spirit matters everything?

I just cannot find it in the Bible. What I find in the Bible – which differentiates our faith from all other world religions – is precisely that *God is to be found in the material*. And that He came to redeem man, soul and body. The Gospel claims the key to all material issues is to be found in the mystery that Christ came in a body, and healed bodies and fed bodies, and that he died in a body, and rose in a body: to save man body and soul.

Christ is the key to every mortal thing.

The baker simply knows that wholemeal bread is better. The farmer simply knows that organic agriculture is healthier. The psychotherapist simply knows that man is a unity, the scientist that this unity is reflected in all nature.

In the meantime, the rest of us simply know that they are all in hopelessly divided compartments. Indeed, we have an uncomfortable feeling that if this now living and explosive matter is left simply in the hands of scientists, then the materialist politician and the materialist scientist will together blow us all up.

The really exciting thing for our day about Christ is that He is the emergent key for all this simple knowing.

At the moment we have left him up a side street as the consoler of the baker in some bereavement, or the comforter of the farmer in some domestic problem, or the stay of the doctor in some operation or decision. We have reduced Christ's ministry to the merely personal. Of course He is all that, but Christ is all that because He is the cosmic key to all life.

Sermon: The Church in the Modern World, April 1948

Nexus

While contemporary faiths insisted that the spiritual was to be discovered in the etheric other-worldly, Christ entered the physical at Christmas to declare the nexus of the spiritual with the material; disparate but conjoined. And, in prophecy, to declare their ultimate reunion in His own Body.

So, while for other faiths such things as slums are matters for regret, but fundamentally passed by, Christ, by taking on our flesh in Bethlehem of Judea, in the reign of Tiberias Caesar, from that moment challenges the rightness of any child being born in untoward surroundings. The physical becomes the only arena for the display of holiness: history ceases to be a long procession of dates and becomes the nave of a Cathedral whose climax is His coming again.

And for that Coming a perpetual exercise is offered us in the availability of the sacrament. But it is an exercise that cannot be lifted from the arena of the physical. Political concern, economic obligation, social betterment and scientific search become not a derivative of our faith, but the stuff of which our faith is moulded, and through which alone our faith can be apprehended.

So seen, healthiness becomes inherent again in Christian holiness, as indeed, when our Bible was translated, the two thoughts were conjoined.

We Shall Rebuild, pp13–14

Holiness and Health

The departmentalising of religion is appalling. It used to be the queen of the sciences, reigning from the throne, with all other forms of knowledge like attendant courtiers working out the ordering of the queen and doing her bidding.

Religion is now the Cinderella of the sciences somewhere in the basement. The two ugly sisters of economics and politics now control the sciences without reference to the children's department downstairs.

This is appalling because the very genius of the Hebrew tradition is its relatedness with all life. In the words of John Macmurray, 'The great contribution of the Hebrews to religion was that they did away with it.' All previous religions had been concerned with the soul and its journey through a negative material order. The Hebrew faith was the first to be concerned with the whole, with the redemption of the material, with the re-creation of the whole person.

That is why Jesus came in a body, incarnate of the Holy Ghost. The

Hebrew tradition in its earliest form expressed it superbly. They were a pastoral people; sheep were their common currency. And it was every morning and every evening that a lamb was sacrificed – a perfect lamb without a blemish.

And who was the celebrant at the sacrifice? Why, the head of the house, the paterfamilias. Their religion was indissolubly interwoven with their daily life. Holiness for them meant health. Indeed Wyclif translated 'knowledge of salvation' as 'science of health'.

That is why I have always been glad that the message of Christmas first came to certain poor shepherds, not attending the midnight service or studying the stars, but in fields as they lay watching their sheep.

If you are going to be very busy today, watching sheep, or mending clothes or typing letters – not mending priest's garments or typing ecclesiastical letters – then rejoice that God may well speak to you first at Christmas time.

Advent talk, December 1958

Holy Child

In Queen Elizabeth's day, to exclaim of an exuberant bairn skipping down the road 'What a holy child!' was not to declare that the child was top of his class in the Sunday School, but simply and totally record that all was well with the child, and that he was honest-to-goodness healthy.

Nor are all these assertions evidenced only by the manner of our Lord's birth. His constant avoidance of the 'sectionally holy' as the place for his ministry; His preoccupation with the fishing and the field, the sheepfold and the market place; His unending concern for the feeding and curing of men's bodies; till, finally, He was content to die between two thieves outside the holy city wall – all witness to the challenge that we must seek again the meaning of His Incarnation.

Sermon, August 1955

God in the Market Place

The Hebrew, and the final and personal Incarnation of all Hebraism, was interested in all life, and met God not in a theological system but in the market place.

Merchants and unemployed queues, judges and debtors, ploughmen and fishermen, rich men and poor men, beggarmen and thieves, men in bed with their children, women on the floor seeking a lost coin – such are the actors on a seemingly quite secular stage which our Lord found a sufficient environment through which to declare to us what He knew about God. Priests and ecclesiastical levies, sacrifices and sabbatical demands He used to point out where the devil might lurk.

Yet because he was God and Man, He none the less conveyed, with consummate art, that the secular was not in itself holy, nor the Temple in essence outmoded. True, when He came to die, outside the Holy City wall, the veil of the innermost Temple was rent from top to bottom. But such was not the end to worship. A New Temple, outside what had come to be holiness, was erected whose altar was His heart, and whose transepts were His outstretched arms of Love. This human edifice was at a world's crossroads where His title had to be inscribed in Hebrew, in Latin and in Greek.

The first congregation for this new dispensation was a thief who cursed Him to the end, another thief who started by cursing and ended by taking communion, and a Roman picket who at least interrupted their own game of cards to accede to His request for a drink. And, three days after, His disciples began to understand what He had meant when He had referred to a New Temple that was His Body.

The dark scene of Calvary is so monstrous that no one of us can bear it for long. Almost unconsciously, as an escape mechanism, we get back into our holy city, stitch up the veil of the temple and begin all over again: with perhaps this concession – that we place an empty cross where the ark of the covenant stood, and so stylise the thieves that they look like the cherubim that were fashioned on that ark.

Thus is 'religion' secured, and we get back to our secular newspapers.

Coracle, March 1956

The Bread of Life

In the sixth chapter of St John's Gospel there is declared the apex of the relationship between the spiritual and the material.

Jesus had fed the multitude, this passage records: and aroused by the grossest of the expectations of the coming of the Messiah – that when he came he would feed everyone – the multitude pursued Him to make Him king. At once Jesus reasserts the spiritual nature of His Kingdom: He is the bread of life in a spiritual sense. But no sooner has He reasserted the spiritual than He uses of Himself the most material language in the whole New Testament. 'Except ye eat the flesh and drink the blood of the Son of Man,' He declares, 'ye have not life in yourselves.' Indeed, the closest translation is 'except ye munch the flesh'. Could there be a more material figure of speech? And yet again, no sooner is it used, than He asserts the spiritual: 'It is the spirit that giveth life, the flesh profiteth nothing.'

The meaning incomparably shines through. The mark of Christian spirituality is to get one's teeth into things. 'I was an hungered and ye gave me meat' … 'Lord, when saw we Thee an hungered?' … 'Inasmuch as ye have done it unto the least of these my brethren.'

Painstaking service in humankind's most material needs is the essence of Christian spirituality. Yet it is only the spirit in which we do things that profits anything.

But further, if we truly get the spiritual view of material actions, a transubstantiation begins to transform the matter itself. As our bodies are the temples of the Holy Spirit, not in the sense of prisons that keep the Spirit captive, but in the sense of designs that can actually be transmuted by the action of the Spirit, so our environment.

Ultimately, in the mystery, this whole earthly creation itself can spiritually be permeated and transformed.

We Shall Rebuild, p116

Every Blessed Thing

Just when the Church of today has confined itself to the 'spiritual' more exclusively than at any time in its history, at that very moment the world of matter has been transformed.

For decades, the Church has gone up the spiritual road, and science has taken over 'the world that matters'. But now, suddenly in our generation, science gives spiritual significance to matter. Einstein summarises it by declaring, 'There is no such thing as dead matter; the ultimate constituents of the atom are light/energy.'

What a moment for the Church! Christ, declares the Gospel, is not just the Light of the Church, or just the Life of the converted soul. He is both because He is the Light and Life of the *world*. In Him everything becomes 'every blessed thing': all becomes vibrant!

Christ could only explain himself in parables. Thus it was that in the Transfiguration His body became vibrant. He became translucent; Moses and Elijah walked with Him; Peter, James and John stood thunderstruck. And Jesus charged them to tell no one until He *rose in a body* from the grave.

Here indeed was manifested the mergence between things spiritual and things material. Christ died and rose in a body to transform the whole body of things.

Christ is vibrant in the material world, not just in the spiritual world.

Mobilisation for Survival

Cosmic Golgotha

Suppose the material order, as we have argued, is indeed the garment of Christ, the Temple of the Holy Ghost? Suppose the bread and wine, symbols of all creation, are indeed capable of redemption awaiting its Christification? Then what is the atom but the emergent body of Christ?

It was on the mountain top that Jesus was transfigured. He spoke with Moses and Elijah in the Ruach (Hebrew for spirit) world, on the mountain top. He was the At-one-ment, the key to the spiritual and the material: unifying love. And His whole body glistened, the preview of His resurrection body.

The Feast of the Transfiguration is August 6th. That is the day when we 'happened' to drop the bomb at Hiroshima. We took His body and we took His blood and we enacted a cosmic Golgotha. We took the key to love and we used it for bloody hell.

Nobody noticed. I am not being cheap about other people. I did not notice it myself. I was celebrating the Feast of the Transfiguration, in a gown and a cassock, a hood, a stole, white hands, saying with the whole Christian ministry, 'This is my body ... This is my blood.'

The while our 'Christian civilisation', without Church protest, made its assertion of the complete divorce between spirit and matter.

One man noticed. When the word came through to Washington of the dropping of the atom bomb – 'Mission successfully accomplished' – Dr Oppenheimer, in large degree in our name its architect, was heard to say, 'Today the world has seen sin.'

Should any reader of this suppose that August 6th, 1945 was Nadir, the lowest point in human disobedience, let us remember that the world potential for perpetrating bloody hell (as 'the lesser of two evils') is now a million times Hiroshima.

Coracle, December 1965

The Garment of Christ

No longer need the scientist strain to hold in unity two contesting lines of thought: one in the area of his intellectual discipline and the other in the area of his morals.

If any reader thinks science speaks contrary to the Faith then let him or her beg or borrow 'Hymn of the Universe' by Teilhard de Chardin. He was brought up in a pious French home to become a Jesuit priest. A brilliant geologist, he followed through that discipline with complete integrity. His awful moment came when he wondered whether in fact it might be true that everything was material and the ancient faith of Christ just pious make-belief: to comfort old ladies and correct young children. He declared that during this period he felt he was encased in an iceberg.

Then the new faith enfolded him, or rather the old half-buried faith came back. This geologist, without giving up an iota of his scientific integrity, knew once more that 'the universe itself is to be freed from the shackles of mortality and enter the liberty of the children of God'.

And this he knew in the Hebrew meaning of that word. For the Hebrew 'to know' is not merely intellectually to perceive, but totally to accept in one's own inner being. As Christ was raised from the dead, so with Teilhard de Chardin, and all who are raised by grace, even now 'are dead and their lives are hid with Christ in God' – body, soul and spirit. And by the same process the whole created order is raised with us.

As the early Celtic saint declared: 'Earth and sea and stars and mankind by that blood are cleansed all.'

Thus Teilhard de Chardin came to speak of the 'Christification of the earth'. In the words of Alice Meynell – of Christ –

Lurking in the cornfield
furtive in the vine
lonely unconsecrated Host.

When Teilhard de Chardin found himself in his geological expedition in the Mongol desert, on the Feast of the Transfiguration, without bread or wine for the celebration of the Mass, he offered up to God the whole universe on the altar of the earth. He was so sure that in prophecy 'every thing cries glory'.

Thus science, in this and every other facet, begins to be seen again not as intellectual knowledge, autonomous in its lostness, but as infinite variations on one theme: the Garment of Christ.

Coracle, December 1965

God in the Material

It is our materialistic world that is throbbing with life today, full of great expectancies.

It is there in psychosomatic medicine, the belief that you cannot divide off man's body from his psyche.

It is there in the cry for wholemeal bread, that is bread with the life put back into it.

It is there in the cry for organic soil culture, the fight against soil erosion, the fight for 'living soil'.

The youth of the world in their unparalleled passion for physical fitness and for new social orders are driven by an imperious conviction that to be whole (that is, to be holy) we must be physically fit in a healthy environment.

It is profoundly urgent that we realise that this is modern materialism: fit subject not for dolefulness but for poetry.

Man has become earthed, one might almost say, only to find God there. It is in this situation that it is madness to try and yank man back into a past age and into the old spiritual constructions.

Surely the job of the Church is, instead, to tell him *that it is God Whom he finds there.*

Science can analyse, science can declare in this department or that – but it cannot give meaning to the whole. And it is profoundly the old Gospel that gives meaning to all their declarations.

Sermon: The Church in the Modern World, April 1948

Redemption of the Body

The lurking doubt in the minds of so many youths that psychology has undermined the essential Christian claim can now be dismissed.

To be sure, psychology has thrown into confusion some of the old concepts of sin. Freud and others have indeed proved that it is not just the evil inclinations of the heart that cause some to fall … It is their hormones gone wrong, their glands out of order. It is their material bodies that have within them the cause of the aberration or perversion that men once called sin.

For the Church simply to continue to command these burdened souls to flog their spirits to bring their bodies into subjection is simply to increase the frustration and hand the victory to the hormones and the glands. There can be no cures in these areas unless we recover a belief in the resurrection of the body: 'We pray God your spirit, soul and hormones and glands may be preserved entire unto the coming of the Lord Jesus Christ.' Not a single sentence of true psychology can be neglected, but it must be seen for what it is, the recovery of bodies for the body of Christ.

Once the redemption of our body is not just part of our intellectual think-ing but takes control of our whole consciousness, we are delivered from a lot of the nonsense that is talked by humanists about the new morality. St Paul, with his doctrine of the body, roundly declares that each of us is a limb of Christ and that it is embarrassing to suggest that the body of Christ should cohabit with a harlot. This makes short shrift of the weary ambiguities of the new morality.

The implication goes far beyond sex and dips into sociology. By the Gospel word, to deal at all with 'the least of these his brethren' is to deal with none other than the body of Christ. Thus the starving Muslim porter on the quay at Singapore is in mystical truth the portrayer, or the prison, of Christ's intention for man.

'Everyman' has significance because Christ died for him, in Singapore or Shetland, be he Buddhist, Baptist or blasphemer. Our concern for his housing and his education become holy activities quite regardless of his colour or his conduct or his religious affiliation.

'Everything,' says Peguy, 'begins in mysticism and ends in politics.'

Coracle, November 1965

The Whole Person

To become a Christian is a total affair, a mind-spirit-soul-and-body affair: a total immersion.

How many, if you were to challenge them – and not just our young people – think of the soul as a captive thing in the cage of our 'neutral' bodies. How much of our preaching indeed is not so addressed to the individual soul, seen as disintegrated from its body? As if the soul of a human being were a canary, beating about in the alien structure of its cage, to be precariously nourished by our words somehow manoeuvred through the bars.

If the soul be a fluttering separated thing, what, in fact, is to be done with it or about it in the multitude of material concerns that affect our weekdays? Immortality becomes a departmental interest, appealing to those who have a peculiar interest in such affairs. And then we wonder why the Church has lost the art of healing!

It is the whole of a person that is immersed in baptism: whether literally or in symbol as far as the ceremony is concerned. It is the whole of a person that goes down to death that the whole of the person may rise. If the Easter promise is a disembodied promise then is our preaching vain.

Yet almost thus are we content; and that at a time when the whole issue of physical fitness is before our youth as not for centuries past. Almost thus are we content – and that at a time when science, through the sheer integrity of its own journeying, is declaring, 'There is no such thing as dead matter' – and are finding, in profoundest truth, that the very mountains skip like rams, the little hills like young sheep, and that even metals have vitality, with the property of 'getting tired'. The whole creation is groaning, as in no previous century, waiting for the revealing of the children of God.

We Shall Rebuild, p58

Living Water

Are you the scientific type? There are three characteristics of scientists, by which you might judge.

They are never satisfied. One of their maxims is 'Be careful, if you think you have found the truth.' Thus the Wise Men went on a long journey, not knowing its outcome.

Then, secondly, they follow one interest. Sometimes they concentrate too much.

The bright young doctor told the old-fashioned general practitioner, 'I'm going to specialise in the nose.'

Said the old man, 'You mean ear, nose and throat.'

'No,' said the youth, 'that is now too vast. I am going to specialise in the nose.'

'Ah,' said the older man, 'and to which nostril do you intend to devote your life?'

Scientists follow one interest. So the Wise Men winnowed down all their science to one small star.

The third mark of the scientist is courage, hazarding thoughts that might make nonsense of everything that was believed before. The Wise Men, like flies in Jerusalem, walked right into the spider's web – Herod's palace – to complete their quest.

Are you the scientific type? Restless, seeking, but concentrating and courageous? Well, Christ comes to you at Christmas.

Follow truth wherever you find it. Even if it takes you outside your preconceived ideas of God or life. Even if it takes you outside your own country into most insignificant alien places like Bethlehem. Be courageous. But concentrate on your search. Truth is one. All roads lead to Home. The seeming devious route will take you to a single star. You will find it is the morning star for you. In the end you will see the Sun behind all suns (as the Celts called Jesus Christ).

And be courageous. Jesus is no static figure. He is the Living Water that follows you through the parched desert. His constancy is in His movement. In the end, moving from the particular, you will find the truth of the general. And you will give Him pre-eminence in all things material, and in all things spiritual – gold and incense. And you will be prepared to die with Him.

Ultimate truth is in Jesus Christ, the Light of the World and its Life.

Advent Talk, December 1958

Man is Made to Rise

Invisible we see You, Christ above us.
With earthly eyes we see above us, clouds or sunshine, grey or bright.
But with the eye of faith we know You reign:
    instinct in the sun ray,
    speaking in the storm,
    warming and moving all Creation, Christ above us.

We do not see all things subject unto You.
    But we know that man is made to rise.
Already exalted, already honoured, even now our
    citizenship is in heaven
Christ above us, invisible we see You.

Invisible we see You, Christ beneath us.

With earthly eyes we see beneath us stones and dust and dross,

fit subjects for the analyst's table.

But with the eye of faith, we know You uphold.

In You all things consist and hang together:

    the very atom is light energy,

    the grass is vibrant,

    the rocks pulsate.

All is in flux; turn but a stone and an angel moves.

Underneath are the everlasting arms.

Unknowable we know You, Christ beneath us.

The Whole Earth Shall Cry Glory

Section four

PRINCIPALITIES & POWERS

All-Matey God

It was a prim little Presbyterian lassie of six years old who was spending her first night away from Scotland with her English aunt. As the aunt kissed her goodnight, she said that she would leave the door open, and the light on in the passage: but also assured her that angels were around her bed.

'Thanks very much, Auntie,' replied pert Miss Calvin, as she pulled the sheet tight to her chin. 'Thanks very much, but we in the Free Kirk never did hold very much with angels.'

Was she perhaps speaking for a little more than the Free Kirk? Was she perhaps speaking generally, however regrettably, for you? Of course, I speak to the believer and not to the cynic. Even in our Lord's time when God spoke to Jesus we read that 'some thought it was an angel, others that it merely thundered'. I speak not to those, ancient or modern, who in every age attribute everything to thunder. But of you, who make room for them in your vocabulary, I ask again, do you in fact experience angels in your present consciousness?

'Invisible we view thee: intangible we touch thee: turn but a stone and start a wing': such may have been the angelic experience of Francis Thompson. But even since his day it is a veritable quarry of stones that has caved in upon our quest: stones too many and too heavy for our lifting before the angel's wing can rustle free.

Add, too, the democratisation of our time! If we have dispensed with a hierarchy round even our earthly national throne: if even at a modern coronation the precedence of dukes and earls, viscounts and barons rise, in our consciousness, as a one-day make-belief: it is foolish to expect, with any realism, a consciousness of a mighty hierarchy round the everlasting throne. Indeed, the democratisation of God is one of the problems of modern faith. In a telling, if vulgar, aphorism someone has suggested that too many today really think of God not as Almighty but rather as all-matey! As if God were but a man: bereft of aura, let alone hierarchy. The weight of materialism, the democratisation of modern man and even of 'God the Ineffable' all militate against our consciousness of angels.

The debits of our time are very great.

Coracle, November 1955

Forward to the Angels

There are credits in our time: and religious credits too. For it is also in the providence of God that angels have receded from our view. If man and his earthly needs reign supreme, in our modern consciousness, it is well not to panic.

With blinding insight the writers of the letters to the Hebrews and to the Ephesians really foresee our day and generation. For they place man in Christ above the angels: above all principalities and powers. It is the fulfilment of humankind that life is about: not only in modern experience but in the purpose of God. And it is to fulfil this overwhelming purpose that increasingly in experience the angels have veiled their faces from our sight. There is no essential need to panic.

But there is every need to be grave. When the Son of Man shall come, shall he find faith on the earth? If Jesus could ask such a question, we must always accept the possibility that our quarry of stones might finally fall in and all thought of angels be smothered by a materialism finally triumphant.

And is it not here that Michael comes in again with all his angels? Yet the cry should not be 'back to the angels' but 'forward to the angels' – How much in their new habiliment, as it were, do we not need them again? We must recover the ancient insight that all forces are ultimately personal, all motions ultimately directed in the service of love, all forms ultimately relatable to the likeness of the Son of Man. That is the first dim vision of a hope.

The second is related. People do not speak of angels today. But behold! They do not hesitate to speak of things demonic: almost they begin to chant 'demonic, demonic' of men and of so-called things. People begin to cringe faithless before powers that they cannot plumb either in the depths beneath or the heaven above.

People are fearful of the unknown in their own make-up. Psychology lays bare that each of us has in one regard the proportion of an iceberg: only the tiny surface of each of us is responsive, so to say, to the wind and weather of our environment. Seven-eighths of each of us is submerged and dark, congealed to the 'group unconscious'.

And man, too, begins to be fearful of the unknown in the marvels around us: fearful of principalities, dominions, powers, such as atomic power: powers as frightening if they became our masters as they would be fruitful kept as slaves. The atom that can only be mysteriously described as light/energy! The force that might alternatively shatter our world to smithereens or shape it into glories yet undreamed!

Coracle, November 1955

War in Heaven

Modern man's fear is all because we have made our God too small: and have lost thereby polarity of thought. Was it Macneile Dixon in his *Human Situation* who averred that before the turn of our century the modern Church placed a seal on the doors of hell: that tolerant man might live more comfortably? Placed a seal on the doors of hell ... only to hear the doors of heaven 'clang-to' in sealed forbidding. We have lost polarity of thought. Demons swarm up, laughing at the futility of our man-made locks. And helplessly we cry 'demonic', and have lost the key to the consciousness of angels again.

It is in this situation, most grave, that I for one do not find it difficult to see, as it were, Michael and his angels rising in new habiliments. There is veritably a war in heaven: in the areas beyond man: in his prison and environment: good and evil forces in eternal combat.

God's whole hope is in man: as adopted sons of Christ. And man, in Christ, must subdue the earth and concentrate on 'matter' to fulfil man's purpose! The angels have withdrawn themselves (increasingly in these many centuries) that man may come into his own: his majesty and birthright. And it is given to our age to see humanity hovering on its fullness. Kings and priests have longed to see the day and have not seen it! And what do we, poor democrats, but 'dive' into matter of spaceships and the deep! How fell is the hour! How frail is modern man! The evil powers beyond man must be held at bay.

Michael and all his angels fight as they have always fought, but in new habiliments. God grant that it will be given to us to see the return of Michael: or, if not to us, to our children: or, if not to them, to our children's children to see the return of Michael. This time not to temples made with hands: but to this emergent universal temple of earth and sky and sea, where everything is heard again to cry 'Glory'.

Coracle, November 1955

Background Music

The fact is we live in a demonic world. At least I hope we live in a demonic world. I hope it is not as reasonable creatures that we spend these astronomical sums on preparing for a war no one can win ... and cannot organise ourselves to spend it on feeding our now united world. If the humanities could do it, surely we would be on the way up by now instead of on the way down.

We have always believed in principalities and powers and the rulers of wickedness in high places. The very essence of our Faith is that we have the answer through our Redeemer.

Michael must come back into our consciousness (not just our intellects). Angels must become our consciousness again ... not floppy damsels in their nighties, but dynamic forces in their serried ranks ... 'the whole company of heaven'.

It is because we have left 'all that' out that the Faith has become 'background music' and demonic secularism rules our souls.

By all means let us say that the secular is the realm of God's activity and that He is in and through all things, but realise He has let loose Satan there, for our disciplining, and that Christ is also there for our salvation.

If there is no darkness there is quite assuredly no Light.

The task is so deep that only a Church with a recovered obedience can hope to cope with it.

Coracle, December 1966

Pentecost

What a wonderful world it is, provided you believe in another world. Not over against our world, but interlaced with it.

The psychologists have got so much the better of us that we look for a rational solution (so called) for everything. The miraculous has been thrown out the window as if it were a department of the abnormal.

In 1963 we had a great occasion on Iona. The Sunday was Pentecost when you remember, in the Bible, all nations understood the Galilean language. The Spirit visited them like a rushing mighty wind.

It was the fourteenth centenary of the coming of St Columba to Iona in 563. Naturally, we made an occasion of it. There were four Moderators there, from Scotland, England, Ireland and Wales. Four bishops, too, from the four nations. And Congregationalists, Baptists, Methodists, Society of Friends, Salvation Army and Greek Orthodox. Christendom in fact was present, not to pray for church unity but to have the sacrament together – certainly the most inclusive communion since the Reformation in Scotland.

I was little more than master of ceremonies, and got up early to get on top of the day. When I got up, I found the carpet in the room was rippling. The windows were not open. The room door was not open.

When I got outside the trees were still, the grasses inert, but there was a howling wind. Pentecost, I said … the rushing of a mighty wind.

As I approached the door of the Abbey, I said to myself, 'This is serious … I have been working too hard … I am getting lightheaded … that is what it is.' The wind immediately stopped. The psychologists had won. I told no one.

After the proceedings were over and the pilgrims were returning to the steamer, a stranger came up to me.

'Have you had any psychic experiences today?' he asked.

I recounted what had happened.

'Ah,' he said, 'this is a well known manifestation of the Spirit.' And he subsequently sent me other examples of the same kind of thing.

Well it had been a bit of a Pentecost, hadn't it? Fourteen nations having holy communion together.

By the way, if you think some door must have been left open, I hope you have a very dull life.

Broadcast talk, 1972

Flight from Reality

Our mental hospitals are full. Our clinics overworked. Our people take aspirin or stronger, the drug that is the dance hall, or embark on an ever quicker tempo of living. Among the more sedate, overfull diaries seek vainly to compensate for hearts that are empty of purpose and minds empty of direction.

'The flight from reality' is the merest cliché for our condition.

'God,' said Augustine more fruitfully, 'has made us for Himself and our hearts are restless till they rest in Him.'

Psychiatry for the moment has donned the dog collar. It has done an immensity of good in the vacuum we have created by our silence. But it is not 'the goods'. Using the longest possible words it is beginning to say again some of the simple things the Faith stands waiting to teach – that there is an individual analysis, for none of us is the same: and that group therapy has a multitude of revelations in store. And what do these two add up to save the play between individual need and congregational recovery with which, in this area, the Church has always been engaged.

The Church of Scotland and the Confessional

Section four

HOLY OBEDIENCE

Born Again

To be 'born again' means exactly what it says.

The emphasis is still on being born: indicative of a process that is still concerned with flesh and blood, still concerned with the concrete problems of this world. But it is still a complete transformation. We have still to deal with material things; but we see them now through the eyes of those who are born of the spirit, and not of those who are born of the will of the flesh.

It is this world we are still concerned with; but we see it differently, and do different things about it. We do not deal with new things instead of old things; but with old things in a new way: indeed all the old 'things' now take on a sacramental significance. 'If any man be in Christ Jesus he is a new creation. The old things are passed away, all things are become new.'

The man of business will attend more, and not less, to his business, and square up to the problems attendant on the fact that his office has now assumed something of the proportions of a holy place. The man of ambition continues to use this attribute of his character (now utterly transformed) for the things of the Kingdom. The man of humour has his humour reborn (not garrotted) and cheers up everyone – no longer just his self-selected clique.

And all forget about haloes and wings, and keep off their coats rather to get into the multifarious activities of converting humanity into Humanity again – not into an anaemic and wholly erroneous imitation of Divinity.

We Shall Rebuild, p55

Space for Wings?

Keeping in touch with God is a concrete experience: as hard as lifting building stones is to the knuckles, as mixing cement is to the fingernails.

One reason why folk fear to indulge in spiritual truths is because of a dangerous misunderstanding of the meaning of the 'spiritual'. Why 'it is so difficult to get men to church' is to be found here. That it was not so difficult in the early centuries was because they knew what we are here saying; and what today is far too seldom portrayed in the actions of the Church. It is our forgetfulness of the Incarnation and what it implies for our whole understanding of the 'spiritual'.

Men erroneously imagine that 'to go mystical' is to turn away from the affairs of this world. They read that they 'must be born again', and imagine it means goodbye to the interests of the world's family; and a consequent giving of such leisure as they can command to mission halls: either singing again the Songs of Zion, or bringing in as many folk as possible, largely to turn their backs on this world's tragic ways.

They think that to be converted is to take off their working coats to leave more space for wings to grow; or their dusty caps to leave free space to let some nebulous halo rise.

The man of humour thinks that, should he become converted, he will have to cultivate solemnity; the man of ambition that he will somehow have to achieve instead an anaemic vacuum as the hallmark of his character. The man of business fears that, if converted, he may have to resign his full-blooded occupation and buy a harmonium the better to play his sacred selections. The young sum up conversion as a series of negatives to be countersigned.

On the whole, men of business, of humour, and of ambition, with their young folk, will have none of it. What they do not know is that Jesus Christ our Lord would have none of it either.

We Shall Rebuild, p54

The Proper Man

For the Garden of Disobedience that was Eden, there is the Garden of Obedience at Gethsemane, obedience wrought out for us at terrible cost by 'The Proper Man'. For the tree of the knowledge of Good and Evil which was the undoing of the first Adam in Eden, there is set up the tree of the new knowledge of Good and Evil, wrought out at terrible cost for our upbuilding by the second Adam.

For the conflict between Cain and Abel, though they were blood brothers, a new filial relationship was set up round the Cross, presented in symbol by the figures of Mary and John. When, from the hour of the Cross, John took Mary to his own home, a new family was set up, no longer after the flesh: but ready now to be composed of all who did God's will; enabled now to be victorious in the doing of God's will through that which had been wrought.

Out of the old conflict into the new; out of the inevitable conflict into a now feasible cooperation; out of the old ways of death into the new ways of life: necessitating being buried with Christ in the waters of His death, that men might rise with Him into a new and corporate life: in a word, being reborn, not of corruptible but of incorruptible seed – such is the essential individual corporate offer of the Gospel, portrayed in the grand processional drama that moves from the Garden of Eden to the Garden of Calvary.

We Shall Rebuild, p28

Tremulous Before God

The whole idea of sin has become vague for our people. Donald Soper says: 'Men used to know themselves as sinners. Now they all think they are victims.' Buchman said: 'Fifty years ago Britishers gave up worrying about sin, since when they have increasingly had to worry about everything else!'

Less and less do we see ourselves as sinners. When some teenage delinquent knocks down an old lady and steals her purse, with one accord we cry that stricter penalties must be applied. Unless the assailant happens to be a distant cousin or lives in our street! Then, of course, we sympathetically suggest that a psychiatrist be called in.

At less violent levels, too, the old conditions that 'made for sin' have been largely mopped up by the welfare state and its genuine benefits. Thus and thus does sin become a mechanical concept in the real mind of many worshippers. Modern people experience a vacuum where our fathers groaned under a conviction of sin.

All this, when truly seen, is an asset on our desert journey. It means we can afford to be more sensitive. The real sins become the subtler ones; and much more like the Bible intention. The grosser sins are being mopped up out of our experience so that we are free to be challenged with the real deadly sins that are more subtle than carnal. We do not yet sufficiently grasp that in our nationalistic complacencies we are blazing sinners, in the New Testament sense of sin.

If we really want to be true to the Reformers in our parallel day, it is not by outward gimmicks, it will be by asking the terrifying questions of *our* time – whether obedience is to be rendered to a Bomb which enforces idolatry and condemns true religion.

Then indeed will we begin to get beyond the gimmicks to the grimness: knock over that pallid table tennis nonsense in the small hall and stand tremulous before God and our obedience for this day. Then indeed Paraphrase 18 will vibrate again and we won't have to fall back on to a 'Communion service set to jazz'. 'Who is on the Lord's side' will become a breathtaking challenge and no longer a half-yawned mumble.

In a word, the Cross becomes central again.

An Idea Whose Hour is Come, pp9–10

The Turning Point

We are not saved by works; but unless we become part of the saving work, salvation ceases to work for us.

We are indeed forgiven our trespasses, but 'if we forgive not men their trespasses neither will our Father in heaven forgive us'. We have, with other citizens of God's Kingdom, been presented with a gold mine, free gratis and for nothing. But we have still got to get picks and go and work the thing – in fear and trembling – if we are to feel enriched.

This 'Christ Rock' that follows us is primarily Comfort (strength), but He is contemporary Commander. Unless we are obedient, we forfeit our salvation. He has a job on. It is the journey of a people. And we have got to 'be Him', together, at whatever point in this desert march happens to be ours.

Now our generation happens to be called to this obedience at a most unique point in human history. We have to show what it means to be obedient 'in Christ' at what future generations are going to call a turning point.

When in Germany, I once gave a lecture on the Fall in the Garden of Eden. Afterwards, a German girl asked me: 'Do you think the atom is the second apple?' I replied: 'Not quite! But all that follows from the harnessing of the atom will cause ultimately a greater Reformation in the Church than the previous one.'

Our basic trouble, which is the reason why the impact of the Church on our country today is so pallid, is that most of our members do not realise how acute is the angle of the turning point we must make.

An Idea Whose Hour is Come, pp4-5

Not Just for a Time

Jesus saves in the measure that we let Him rule always and not just for a time. In the measure that we are enslaved to Him always and not just for a time.

You just try it in these coming days – I am not pleading because you have already, in fact, made up your mind to do so – just try being a Wise Man this Christmas.

Bring the gold to Him. Offer Him the material world in which you move, and run it on human lines.

Bring the incense to Him. Offer Him your spiritual life, your instincts and desires, lay them at His feet. It is easy at Christmas when the spirit of Give is everywhere about.

And, if you want His way to rule, and His love to save, not just for a time, then offer Him myrrh, the symbol of burying.

Kill your old self. Keep the world turned upside down just for His sake, and you will find that Jesus comes to save – not just for a time.

Advent Talk, December, 1958

The New Style

To make Christian holiness very much a matter of fact is at once to demand a more costly exercise of prayer and a more costing reading of the Bible than any more partial approach demands.

The 'devotional' reading of the Bible which (old style) used to be connected in folks' minds with such a text as 'O, for the wings of a dove, that I might fly far away' from mundane concerns, is not really achieved (new style) till we have got through to the very matter of fact and extremely costing demand that it makes in our mundane lives.

The 'devotional' reading, say, of the Christmas story (old style) meant contemplation on the glory of angels' voices and the beauty of the Mother and the Babe amidst the lowing cattle – prior to going back to do our best in the workaday world. New style, this reading has not got through till we are uncomfortably confronted with the fact that still a considerable proportion of the babies in Glasgow are born in conditions worse than in any city in Europe, and the even more uncomfortable fact that such is not the affair mainly of the sanitary department, but happens also to be an affair of the angels.

The new style dictates that we are not doing our best in the workaday world until we are doing something to put that right. The idea that practical social concern is in danger of being too much an affair of 'works' and that our 'real job' is Bible reading and prayer emerges as a hopeless confusion of the facts.

It is the practical social concern that makes prayer spring into life. Thus folk who accept the challenge of the Incarnation are forced to prayer – long and earnest prayer, not just about practical social concerns, indeed not mainly about practical social concerns, but rather about their own relationship to God, about the kind of ways in which God acts, about their own unworthiness to criticise anyone else, if they are not to fall into being semi-Christian social agitators who annoy by their own self-righteousness and depress by their ineffectiveness.

We Shall Rebuild, pp128–9

All Labour is Holy

'What do you do as a Christian?' a perfervid evangelist asked a fellow traveller in the train.

'I bake,' said the man.

'Yes, that is your profession; but what do you do as a Christian?'

Refusing all openings to admit that, as a Christian, he taught in the Sunday School or preached at the street corner or distributed tracts, the man persisted in the sufficiency of the reply – that he baked.

He was right. Such is the centrality of the Incarnation faith. Teaching, preaching, works of mercy are the periphery: essential, but periphery.

The carpenter, the fisherman, the agriculturalist – or, if you will, the miner, the ironworker and the aeroplane craftsman – are God's final revelation of His purpose in creation, in the Lord Jesus Christ of the carpenter's shop at Nazareth, of the fishing fleet at Galilee, and of the home at Bethany. It is the truth of that which it is the Christian mission to declare till all labour is holy and every home His temple.

Yet, in the paradox, so to salt the daily round and the common task we must be separate. Unless in our 'involvement' we be separate, homes become adulterated, farm land becomes exploited, and aeroplanes mount guns: all of which is happening before our eyes.

We Shall Rebuild, p118

Following the Rock

In this boiling sea of mutual fears which is our world environment today, what does it mean to 'go to Christ'? Is Christ a sort of steady rock in the middle of the whirlpool? Does conversion mean to be enabled to clamber onto that rock and know your safety in Him, whatever hurricane may blow? Any such limited interpretation sounds remarkably like 'saving your own life'. This, our Lord assures us, is the one way of losing your life, of being damned.

Most of us know it does not mean that, but it is well to face the fact that multitudes outside the Church think that such is what we exist to be and to do – just a bunch of escapists.

What then does it mean to 'come to Christ'? Well, it is still coming to a Rock: but to a mysterious one. When Israel, with its destiny to become God's people, moved through the wilderness of Sinai, the Rock that followed them was Christ. His stability resides in His movement. He is not static but alive. He walks on the stormy sea and faith means joining Him there: and, in His strength, commanding the tempest.

He is Comforter, but He is also Commander. It is true that He rids us of our frustration, without any assistance on our part. What really 'unmans' mankind from doing much about the Bomb is that we all know we too are rotten to the core. We are each tiny replicas inside of the conflict that forms our environment. 'All our righteousnesses are as filthy rags': even the good jobs we do in Church and business and trades unions, to help and serve them, are themselves all shot through with false motives.

With this Original Crack-Up in all of us, we believe Christ has dealt. He made on the Cross, once and for all, the at-one-ment between our ideals and our make-up. In the Resurrection, His Spirit was united with His body. We believe in the Resurrection of the body. New Creatures we become.

An Idea Whose Hour is Come, p4

A Costly Business

There was a terrible drought in Canada. If rain didn't come at once, thousands would be ruined. So the word passed around that the next afternoon there would be a service in church to pray for rain to come at once.

From long distances God's faithful people drove in, in their buggies, their two-wheeled dogcarts, their Fords, their Morrises and their Land-Rovers. But here is a strange thing – *only one person brought an umbrella.* Why? Because she expected it to rain, and she was a little child.

In other words, there was only one really faithful person there. She really believed, as we would say, that God would answer prayer. Her faith was declared in an act.

I happen to deal with senior ex-Reformatory boys. They come to me often, I am afraid, when they are broke. I suppose they think I have faith in them. One came to me because he had the offer of a job a hundred miles away, but he would require a railway ticket, overalls and money for a week's lodgings till his pay came in. For landladies, bless them, are almost bound to live by sight and not by faith. But we are the family of faith … what was I to do?

Now I don't doubt it would be prudent to go to the railway station and buy his ticket, and his overalls, and tell the minister at the destination to fix up and pay for the lodgings. Yes, it would be prudent, but one thing is certain – I would not have faith in that boy and, of course, it is faith in him that is what he needs to cure him.

If we are to be made free by faith in Jesus Christ, if we are to be justified by faith, it means acting now as if this world was Jesus' world. It means a costly business, living by faith and not by sight, costly in cash, costly in reputation. It means often being done down by life in order to rise in life. And I suggest it is precisely that for which we are not very famous. And I suggest that is also why we are not carefree.

Act as if Jesus ruled now. And as you pray for God to pour down His mercy on you, you had better take a pretty stout umbrella. Firstly, because if you really act in faith, a lot of people will throw things at you, and secondly, because you will feel such a spring shower of forgiveness coming down on you that it will soak you!

But at last you will feel carefree, you will feel justified by faith, not in a textbook sense but in an overwhelming sense.

Sermon, August 1953

Spiritual Authority

A general during the war was sitting in a first-class carriage which was quite full, save for one seat. His moustaches could be heard faintly bristling behind a *Daily Telegraph*.

Enter a leading aircraftsman, uncommissioned, but dead tired. He swung his webbing on the rack and slumped into the vacant seat. Enter from the corridor a young and whippersnapper Captain.

'Give me that seat, young man,' he said to the aircraftsman. 'It's an order.'

The order was obeyed: the aircraftsman withdrew into the corridor.

Then, from behind the *Daily Telegraph* the steady bristling of the moustache assumed almost the crackle of a forest fire.

'Give that man back his seat,' the general said with immense authority. The whippersnapper demurred.

'It's an order,' roared the general. The order was obeyed. The whippersnapper withdrew into the corridor. And out into the corridor came the general.

'Now,' he said to the whippersnapper, 'you take my seat and I'll stand out here.'

The crestfallen captain demurred.

'It's an order,' said the general, and stood outside the rest of the journey.

That is what is meant by spiritual authority.

Bombs and Bishops, pp5–6

Recovery of Persons

We wonder if the world has meaning, whether everything may not be accidental and chaotic.

A man went into a picture gallery. He walked round the room where all the old masters were.

When he came out he said to the janitor, 'I don't think much of your old masters.'

'Sir,' said the janitor, 'it is not the old masters that are on trial here.'

The book of Revelation assures us that the Kingdom of God is not a 'mayhap' or a 'maybe'. It is not really for us to make judgement about the Kingdom of God. The Kingdom of God *is*. It is you and I who are on trial. The heavenly city is assured – four square, majestic and certain. If we attack it, then like Don Quixote we simply break our lance. It is in the light of this certain principle that we must live our lives.

But not only must we accept this principle, conveyed by the city. We must recover persons.

The ultimate city is not a static blueprint. It is not a pagoda for a priest.

The final community is pre-eminently personal.

I think it is desperately important for our contemporary obedience to get this clear. Our world is getting dangerously impersonal.

Sermon, December 1963

By Proxy

If you find it difficult to picture a final coming of Christ, will you join with me in preparing for His coming by proxy?

Jesus gave us a parable of the final judgement. He gave us the rules whereby we can be ready for His coming.

If we are not to be ashamed at the Judgement, we are to feed the hungry, release people in prison and comfort the depressed. And why? Because inasmuch as we do it to the least, we do it to Him.

Modern that we are, we may not be able to visualise the final Jordan to be crossed. But we are crossing tributary streams every day which all go to swell the final Jordan.

At the last we will meet Jesus. But we meet Him every day by proxy – in all the hungry, imprisoned, depressed folk that we meet.

Sermon, December 1959

The Way of the Cross

Am I unbalanced when I declare my conviction that our secular world is very near the Eleventh Hour?

For fourteen hundred years the centric witness of the Church has been that rough justice can only be maintained if Christians are prepared in the last instance to go to war. It was the ec-centric witness (off-centre witness) which declared that there is a power in the Way of the Cross for society as for individual people.

Am I unbalanced to suggest that the Way of the Cross must now become the way of society in our already united world, as for personal relations? This is now centric. It is now the eccentric Christian (in the strict and colloquial sense) surely who supposes justice can be defended or established by modern war.

Suppose it is the Church that alone can bring peace to the world by exalting the Cross right now?

If this is really so, we have a long way to go. At the moment, the institutional Church is completely submerged in this particular chaos.

A missionary in India with great courage decided to accompany the pagan tribe of his district on the occasion of their annual pagan festival. He marched with them into the forests by night till they came to the point where they paused to go down to the groves for their obscenities and bestialities. At the moment of the pause he preached the love of God. The young men nearly killed him for his interference. But he returned to his compound, to his surprise, unscathed. The next year he repeated the act and there was a lessened tension. For nine consecutive years he repeated his preachment on the great occasion, just before the tribe went down into the dirt. Then he died a natural death. The next year when the feast came round, the head of the tribe asked the mission to send someone else *because it had now become part of the show.*

Our secular world is bankrupt when it isn't perpetuating the obscenities. The Church, in this regard, is part of the show.

Most assuredly it is not a new preoccupation with the things of peace that will revive us. The Bomb is not God's trick to recover His institutional Church. But a faithful obedience to the Way of the Cross, for the twentieth century, can do no other than take account of our modern plight and see faithlessness as the cause of our secular world.

Coracle, December 1966

The Cross

I simply argue that the Cross be raised again at the centre of the market place as well as on the steeple of the church. I am recovering the claim that Jesus was not crucified in a cathedral between two candles, but on a cross between two thieves; on the town garbage heap; at a crossroad so cosmopolitan that they had to write his title in Hebrew and in Latin and in Greek (or shall we say in English, in Bantu and in Afrikaans?) at the kind of place where cynics talk smut, and thieves curse, and soldiers gamble.

Because that is where He died. And that is what He died about.

Only One Way Left, p38

Section six

THE REDEEMED
COMMUNITY

Germinating Centre

The Bible is all about community: from the Garden of Eden to the city at the end. From the family that in Eden fell, through the reconstituted Israel, its apex in Judah, its fulfilment in Christ, its manifestation in Pentecost, its fellowship in the Acts and its expectation of ultimate peace round the Lamb that once was slain, the Bible is all about community.

The Bible takes man's natural search for community to remake it entirely. It does so through Christ who was slain before all worlds, manifest in history, and who, in St Paul's inexpressible vision, when all things are subject unto Him, 'shall Himself be subject unto God who put all things under Him that God may be all in all'.

The Bible declares the failure of all lesser communities and the nature of this redeemed community by which all others will some day be encompassed or condemned.

This community is already secured for us in the person of Jesus Christ, the Man who intercedes before the throne. The condition of our continuing security is that we retain alike the vision of ourselves already lifted up, our citizenship in heaven, and the obligation to be His body on earth, His embassy in history. We are the germinating centre of His purpose. He is the Light of the world. We are the Light of the world.

Only One Way Left, pp146–7

No Other Plans

There is a very old legend, and all legends that persist speak truth, concerning the return of the Lord Jesus Christ to heaven after His Ascension.

It is said that the angel Gabriel met Him at the gates of the city.

'Lord, this is a great salvation that Thou hast wrought,' said the angel.

But the Lord Jesus only said, 'Yes.'

'What plans hast Thou made for carrying on the work? How are all men to know what Thou hast done?' asked Gabriel.

'I left Peter and James and John and Martha and Mary to tell their friends, and their friends to tell their friends, till all the world should know.'

'But, Lord Jesus,' said Gabriel, 'suppose Peter is too busy with his nets, or Martha with her housework, or the friends they tell are too occupied, and forget to tell their friends – what then?'

The Lord Jesus did not answer at once; then He said in His quiet, wonderful voice: 'I have not made any other plans. I am counting on them.'

Govan Calling, p115

The Embassy

Because Christ came not to condemn the world, but that the world through Him might be saved, so, though our citizenship – our true life – is already in heaven, we have a work to do on earth. Incorporate in Him, we have, as His instruments, a world to save. 'Christ has no hands now but our hands, no feet but our feet, ours are the eyes with which He looks out in compassion on the world' (St Teresa).

This is our calling: that is the Church. This or that local congregation, this or that general assembly of the saints, is an embassy in an alien land, representing the dictates of the King to whose heavenly court we already belong. Like this world's embassies, which used to be built actually on soil carried from the home country, our very church buildings are, so to say, built on heavenly soil.

To grasp this offer, to accept a place in this New Community, is to glimpse the reason for the extravagant language of the early fathers. One of them called the Christian experience 'that divine intoxication more sober than sobriety itself'.

And corporate Christian worship involves the declaration of our Faith that all this is true; the confession of our failure to live in the light of it; the renewing of our incorporation in Him and with each other; the giving of thanks that death for us is passed; the receiving of instructions of what we are to do with our hands, our feet and our eyes that the world may feel and know His compassion; and the acceptance of His blessing on us in what together we go out to do in Him and for Him in winning back His world.

We Shall Rebuild, p29

Community of Sinners

It is time for us to tell the outsider that the Church is not composed – and never has been – of people who think they are good. In actual fact it is composed of the only people left in the world who happen to know we are bad; that we ourselves bear some of the responsibility for the selfishness that is ruining the world; and that we cannot get ourselves right.

The Church is composed of the people who have accepted the thesis that something once happened to the world – to set at naught our disability – through the obedience of the one man who was the only 'Proper Man'; and have accepted His offer to engraft us into Himself whereby alone we too can begin to become proper men: through Him to grow into something less manifestly selfish than we used to be.

Thus we go to Church every Sunday, firstly to say openly – and anyone who wants to can come and hear us – that we are sinners and might just as well be blotted out; but also to claim forgiveness, and to declare our faith that we can start again together in Him, cleansed and empowered.

In a world so increasingly unhappy that ever more people – to make it bearable – imagine themselves to be victims, believers are those who, instead, admit that they are sinners; but who claim and experience a way out, through One who voluntarily became the victim. So to believe is to find deliverance for good from all the weariness attendant on this modern, everlasting, mutual blame of one another. To act in this belief is to put people in the way of their conversion.

We Shall Rebuild, pp52–3

Mystical and Material

History conjoined with Mystery is the challenge of the Gospel. History degenerates into a fog of dates and meaningless tragedy unless we enlighten it with the claim that God has entered into it.

But the mystery of God ascends into the ethereal, impenetrable cloud, unless we accept the delineation of Himself in the historic person of Jesus Christ, 'the express image of the Father'. It is perpetually to keep in mind the triumphant drama of the angels, both descending and ascending, that alone can save us from making of life a tragedy. And He that descended is the same as He that hath ascended. Our prayers must be about earthly things, even as the answers are about heavenly things. Jesus Christ is the interpreter both of God and of history: in Him is the Atonement. And those who are His must be, simultaneously, very mystical and very material.

All the times of declension that the Church has known can be attributed either to a preoccupation with the mystical, to the exclusion of earthly concerns; or to a preoccupation with history to the exclusion of things that are not seen. The socialists who say, 'The Church should drop all its fuss about worship and champion the cause of the working man,' are as wrong as the churchmen who say, 'It's no good worrying about the social order till we have got folk converted.'

All times of true revival in the Church have occurred when a return has been made to Jesus Christ, who never allows us to be content with exclusive mystic contemplation or exclusive earthly preoccupation. Our present tragedy, with 'one world dying and the other powerless to be born', is that the Church is too ethereal in its instructions, and the world too material in its constructions. Jesus Christ, the God-Man, is the mystery that can alone make plain our world.

We Shall Rebuild, p51

Being a Human

The 'Atonement' makes it possible to declare that the unique mark by which the Divine Society that is the Church should be recognised is its fundamental, honest-to-goodness *humanity*.

And is not this what our congregational life in the main requires? How often are church social activities dehumanised; either straining after a false piety so that it is a relief for everyone (in their hearts) to get away, or so indistinguishable from the multitude of sub-human secular fellowships everywhere about that we might as well have stayed at home.

Some of us remember the first fortnight of the Iona Community in 1938, when a group composed of craftsmen and clergymen found themselves pledged to live together the Faith, as applied not to leisure hours but to the whole round day, erecting the first huts. It was a terrific strain!

All the parsons, including the writer, were concerned to show ourselves by our every act 'he-men', 'natural', not high-falutin, good carpenters. The intention was right; but we were doing it to be seen of men. What was worse was the constant effort of the craftsmen to behave in terms of what they presumed to be the essential attributes of parsons! We had known them long before as natural and intimate friends. But what a transformation was now upon them!

They were in a 'religious community' so they must be 'different': walk softly; mention no conceivable subject on which anyone might with passion differ; laugh moderately, after full assurance that it was a laughing matter; and move generally as if some grapeshot had lodged in their spine and never been removed.

Only a row could clear such mutual artificiality. And after it we became a community of very ordinary men, who knew it, said it, and thereby began to grow. Only with such a fellowship can God do anything at all.

The thing is a parable. Our congregations miss the zest of the early Christian Church because we have forgotten the glorious emancipation of our true humanity that was the Incarnation. Jesus the carpenter, the friend of shepherds and fishermen, showed us God by being human – and in three days set at naught the complex temple that was forty years in building. He made risen humanity His temple. We must be human.

We Shall Rebuild, pp55–6

The Master Builder

In Iona, to get rightly weathered stones for the rebuilding, we are at pains to pull down old walls in the vicinity – the property of the Church – to find the original boulders.

Sometimes we come on greater quarry: an actual freestone window ledge, or carved coping, still bearing the mason's marks and the fashioning of long ago. A few of these we have built back into the very niche from which they fell, three to four hundred years ago.

114

It contains a thought. In our natural lives we are undirected stones, still short of our destiny. Even a stone becomes itself when it is shaped and used. To be baptised is to be chosen out, to be marked by the Master Builder, and to be fashioned for a place of His appointing in that living temple of which He is also the chief corner stone. Nor, if the choosing-out has been authentic, can we ever permanently fall away.

We may get lost in secular constructions for long enough, the marks of our true purpose hidden at least from mortal eyes. But we can always be built back.

We Shall Rebuild, p59

Living Temple

It is difficult for us modern people to understand the Second Coming of Christ. It is more difficult for us than it was for our fathers.

They lived in a miraculous age, so much unknown, so much mysterious. We live in a mechanical age, so much is cut and dried. But can we see how to prepare for Him, in ways that a modern mind can understand?

Nearly a thousand years ago, almost the whole of Christendom believed in a literal understanding of the book of Daniel. So they believed Christ was coming back to judge the world when the thousand years were over. As they came near to a thousand years ago, they said, 'Jesus will be returning soon now.' In such a mood, you might reasonably suppose that they ceased to care for what was happening around them.

But the opposite was the case. Believing He would be coming soon, what happened was feverish activity ... in starting to build the great cathedrals which have stood completed these last thousand years.

Why on earth, you might ask literally, did they build cathedrals when they thought the earth would soon be consumed? The answer always moves me. It was because they wanted Jesus to have a beautiful place to come to.

Perhaps we don't think in that literal way today. Perhaps we think more of people than of places in our day. Perhaps we don't think of a temple made with hands, but rather a living temple of people with each of us as living stones, and Christ Jesus as the corner stone: of a community rather than a stone construction.

And I rather think we are right.

What we should be doing is to build more beautiful societies for Him to come to. A more beautiful Glasgow with fewer slums. A more beautiful Africa, with fewer shanty towns.

So that if He came, we would feel less ashamed of our failure in fellowship.

Sermon, December 1959

A Movement, Not a Meeting House

The nature of the new order will be revealed not by the searchlight of high-powered brains, but in response to the obedience of convinced persons ... For Christ is a person to be trusted, not a principle to be tested. The Church is a movement, not a meeting house. The faith is an experience, not an exposition. Christians are explorers, not map makers. And the new social order is not a blueprint which someone must find as soon as possible. It is a present experience made possible at Bethlehem, offered on Calvary and communicated at Pentecost.

Christ is the light of the world and the life of the world. He is the light-energy for our individual needs because He is the key to the ultimate nature of all existence ... He is the only interpreter, but the quite sufficient interpreter, of our modern impasse. He must somehow be declared again to the physical consciousness, the scientific inquiry and the social passions of modern man ... It was God who made modern man a materialistic creature: and that far from stultifying our witness, materialism opens a new and effectual door if only we preach the full old Gospel.

Sermon, August 1955

All Healing is of God

Healing is a central obligation of the Church. Christ came neither to save souls nor to save bodies. He came to save people. Thus our whole ministry is one of healing: making crooked places straight in international issues, in class issues, and issues of sex. In Christ Jesus there is neither Jew nor Greek, bond nor free, male nor female. He is the At-one-ment. And as of the larger, so of the less. Christ makes crooked people straight. As in the body politic, so in the human body He makes straight, here the crooked mind and there the crooked body, and most often the crooked mind-body.

Just as there is no such thing as 'Christian Truth' over against Truth, so there is no such thing as 'Christian Healing' over against Healing. All healing is of God, and the man who walks again after penicillin is just as much divinely healed as a man who walks again after a service of the laying on of hands. We have no divine repository where 'religious' things happen over against a hospital where so-called merely physical things happen.

We must avoid the danger of 'separateness' – the tendency to concentrate on divine healing as if it can be an isolated recovery, sealed off from social concern. It comes, for instance, somewhere near blasphemy that we should merely pray for 'Margaret, suffering from TB', when we know quite well this illness was contracted in a damp room in the slums of Glasgow. This is not to say that we dare not pray for Margaret till all slums have been cleared. For God is a father, and not just an indifferent guardian of righteousness. He is a God of mercy who saves and heals, while we are yet sinners. But it is to say that it is near blasphemy merely to pray for her individually when there is a known cause which we should be tackling at the same time.

If the Church should ever come to say, 'We have tried missions and little comes of them; we have concerned ourselves with politics but only got into a mess; we have read psychology but it is all so complex; let us "go to": here is a straight run through: we will become very consecrated, very "spiritual": we will escape the Cross of history and embrace the offer of individual resurrections': then we will have succumbed to a reversion. Nor will we be rewarded. Having fasted, having bowed our heads as bulrushes, God in fact will not listen, nor will He hear.

Coracle, October 1954

118

The Fellowship

Our modern environment makes clearer for us, than for many previous generations, the real nature of our task. We must become more separate and more involved.

This, as an abstract theory, sounds so meaningless that the only way to achieve it is to become personally committed to Christ – the essence of whose mysterious Person is precisely that He was both. He is the end of the conflict between our ideals and our instincts. He is the key.

But His plan is not that a number of separate persons must become united with Him and in mutual isolation be His instruments for the redemption of the world. His instrument is a fellowship, His continuing mystical body on earth, in which we are members incorporate.

It is this outgoing and outgiving organism that He has created for the saving of the world. Constant and corporate mission belongs, therefore, to the essence of the Church's life. And it is the nature of her corporate separatedness and corporate involvement that we must find again.

We Shall Rebuild, p97

The Inner Building

Come it soon or come it late, the future of the community lies in the recovery of our substantial, and no longer rarefied, Faith.

'If Christ be not risen from the dead, then are we of all men the most miserable.' For science then has no North Star by which to steer its course. Psychology turns in upon itself and turns morality into a morass. Sex seeks to become its own reward, for there is no longer any meaning in 'procreation', as the loveliest delegation ever given by a Father to His children. And sociology becomes the plaything of the materialist.

Iona can be the home of the New Reformation. But it must recover its genius: keep acting its insights at whatever risk if its insights are to be clarified and the next obedience seen. If, as a community, we write at all it can be no more than passing calculations in the sand, to point to the next obedience.

We must fill our liturgy on the island with the knowledge of what it is we handle when we handle Bread and Wine.

We must 'come out from amongst' those who would turn our Faith into a relativity, or who would turn our Resurrection absolute into an amiability towards all. Indeed we must serve all, to the point of death, and welcome every faith and every failure because we know in what image they were originally made.

We must enter the issues of international monetary policy as just as urgent for solution as any housing or educational obligation. And through it all must be the new community of non-violent and yet utterly involved obedience. It is the inner building now that challenges.

If this be more than words then our Church 'has a baptism to be baptised with and how shall we be straightened till it be accomplished'.

New techniques entirely of the nature of the devotional life will need to be forged. Such can only be forged by those who continue at any cost to be involved in the world as it is.

Coracle, December 1965

A Great Mystery is Your Church

Almighty God;
we bless You for the mystery of the Church.
No human society is she, striving to be like You.
No accidental throwing together of struggling humans is she.
She is bone of Your bone and flesh of Your flesh.
She is Your substantiation here on earth.
A great mystery is Your Church.
We did not choose to be Your heralds and to be Your defenders.
You chose us: and named us and appointed us to bear fruit.
A great mystery is Your Church.

Nor did You choose us because we are a great people:
it is clear for anyone to see that we are the least of all people.
You have put Your love upon us because You love us –
a great mystery is Your Church.

You died on Calvary: to rise again and reign now.

And we were buried with You in the waters of baptism

that with You we might rise to newness of life.

We are already dead, and our lives are hid with You.

The undertakers have been and gone for us.

Our citizenship is already in heaven.

We are just Your ambassadors here

to represent You in a fallen world.

It's all so strange: but You made it like that.

The Whole Earth Shall Cry Glory

Postscript

There are only three Resurrection crosses in Scotland. They show Christ on the Cross, not naked with a Crown of Thorns, but robed in splendour as a king: reigning from the Cross. The Divine Majesty is sufficiently revealed in the suffering Humanity!

In our day, man is coming into his own. Is it to kill himself, or to find his true stature in Christ?

An Idea Whose Hour is Come

Index

Index contd.

About Ron Ferguson

After seven years in journalism, Ron Ferguson studied in the UK and USA, where he received the degree of Master of Theology from Duke University. He was deputy warden of Iona Abbey from 1980–81, and was then elected Leader of the Iona Community from 1981–88. He is now minister of St Magnus Cathedral, Orkney and a regular columnist with *The Herald*. The author of several books, his biography of George MacLeod (see opposite) was shortlisted for the prestigious McVitie's Scottish Writer of the Year Award when first published.

Also from Wild Goose Publications ...

THE WHOLE EARTH SHALL CRY GLORY
Iona prayers
George MacLeod

Poems and prayers by the Iona Community's founder interspersed with images of the island.

'To be in a seat at Iona Abbey, to be moved by the awesome oratory of a MacLeod sermon in full flood, to be led into the nearer presence of God by means of kaleidoscopic, imaginative prayer, is to be privileged and – more importantly – to be changed.'

Ron Ferguson, former Leader of the Iona Community

1985 · 64pp · 0 947988 01 7 · £5.99

GEORGE MACLEOD
A biography
Ron Ferguson

A full and detailed account of the life of this heir of a famous ecclesiastical dynasty, during which he became disillusioned with the status quo and moved inexorably towards socialism and pacifism in his life and work as a minister.

Realising that radical moves were necessary to meet the needs of the times, George MacLeod embarked on the imaginative venture of rebuilding part of the ancient abbey on the Isle of Iona, taking with him unemployed craftsmen from the shipyards of the Clyde and trainee ministers, whom he persuaded to work as labourers. Out of this was born the often controversial Iona Community, which over the years has developed innovative forms of worship, pleaded for disarmament, inveighed against world hunger and advocated joint ecumenical action on social issues.

272pp approx. · 1 901557 56 1 · £10.99 approx. · Summer 2001

The Iona Community

The Iona Community, founded in 1938 by the Revd George MacLeod, then a parish minister in Glasgow, is an ecumenical Christian community committed to seeking new ways of living the Gospel in today's world. Initially working to restore part of the medieval abbey on Iona, the Community today remains committed to 'rebuilding the common life' through working for social and political change, striving for the renewal of the church with an ecumenical emphasis, and exploring new, more inclusive approaches to worship, all based on an integrated understanding of spirituality.

The Community now has over 240 Members, about 1500 Associate Members and around 1500 Friends. The Members – women and men from many denominations and backgrounds (lay and ordained), living throughout Britain with a few overseas – are committed to a fivefold Rule of devotional discipline, sharing and accounting for use of time and money, regular meeting, and action for justice and peace.

At the Community's three residential centres – the Abbey and the MacLeod Centre on Iona, and Camas Adventure Camp on the Ross of Mull – guests are welcomed from March to October and over Christmas. Hospitality is provided for over 110 people, along with a unique opportunity, usually through week-long programmes, to extend horizons and forge relationships through sharing an experience of the common life in worship, work, discussion and relaxation. The Community's shop on Iona, just outside the Abbey grounds, carries an attractive range of books and craft goods.

The Community's administrative headquarters are in Glasgow, which also serves as a base for its work with young people, the Wild Goose Resource Group working in the field of worship, a bi-monthly magazine, *Coracle*, and a publishing house, Wild Goose Publications.

For information on the Iona Community contact:
The Iona Community, Pearce Institute, 840 Govan Road,
Glasgow G51 3UU, UK. Phone: 0141 445 4561
e-mail: ionacomm@gla.iona.org.uk   web: www.iona.org.uk

For enquiries about visiting Iona, please contact:
Iona Abbey, Isle of Iona, Argyll PA76 6SN, UK.
Phone: 01681 700404   e-mail: ionacomm@iona.org.uk